# JENNY BRISTOW'S

## COUNTRY COOKING

**2**

# JENNY BRISTOW'S

## COUNTRY COOKING

### 2

MOUTH-WATERING HOME-STYLE RECIPES
FROM AROUND THE WORLD.

APPLETREE PRESS

First published in 1997 by
The Appletree Press Ltd
19–21 Alfred Street
Belfast  BT2 8DL

Tel:  +44 (0) 1232 243074
Fax: +44 (0) 1232 246756
email:frontdesk@appletree.ie

Jenny Bristow's Country Cooking 2

A catalogue record for this book
is available from The British Library.

ISBN  0-86281-697-1

website:www.irelandseye.com

9 8 7 6 5 4 3 2 1

# Contents

# Introduction

**Jenny Bristow's Country Cooking 2**, is the follow up
to the book which accompanied the television series,
**Country Cooking 1**. As with the previous book I have
taken the best of the produce from around the world,
brought it back home and used it to create many new,
lively dishes based on each individual country's way
of cooking. What I found so interesting was that so
many of these so called foreign foods produce dishes
that are fresher, livelier in flavour, and healthier, with
shorter cooking times and totally in tune with our
modern way of life.

The cuisines of the world are so varied and vast, but
this is not a book about foreign or fancy cookery,
instead it shows how to use our new found
ingredients, in clever ways that will appeal to
everyone: families, meatless eaters, singles, students,
those with little time to cook or shop, or if it's
something for a special occasion that you are looking
for, then I know you will find many new
ideas here.

This time I have visited Australia, in *The Foods from
Down Under,* and discovered clever ways to use the
kiwi fruit, in a Kiwi Lime & Coconut Chicken that
I know you will just love.

In *The Mexican Way* I have introduced heat - hot chillies and spices into our own way of cooking and made a casserole with the heat turned up, and a healthy Citrus Chicken dish with hardly a trace of fat. In *Savouring Spain* the traditional Sunday lunch with pork fillet is cooked Mediterranean style with couscous, sherry, honey and olive oil, then served with hot salads. In *Glorious Greece* you will almost feel you have been transported to the Greek Islands, with sun-drenched recipes that use summer berries topped with thick, creamy, luxurious yoghurt, or chicken cooked with walnuts in the most delicious sauce I have ever tasted. *The Flavours of France* are sophisticated yet the techniques are simple, to produce sauces, soufflés and an almond scented pear and cinnamon tart served with Chantilly cream. When it comes to Christmas, you will discover more and more that foods from abroad influence what we cook for our families at Christmas: All American Spiced Turkey, with a Fruit & Nut stuffing, the Moroccan way to flavour a pork and dried fruit casserole, and the eastern influence in a stuffing for a turkey breast.

To complete my culinary journey I came back home and in *Home Grown*, cooked with great pride local produce: Irish Salmon wrapped in Herbs, Bramley Apples to make the Apple of my Eye Pie, and in true Irish fashion made an Irish Stew with no lamb - but with a fishy flavour instead.

# Conversion of Measurements

## Temperature

| Temp°C | Temp°F | Gas Mark |
|--------|--------|----------|
| 110 | 225 | $\frac{1}{4}$ |
| 120 | 250 | $\frac{1}{2}$ |
| 140 | 275 | 1 |
| 150 | 300 | 2 |
| 160 | 325 | 3 |
| 180 | 350 | 4 |
| 190 | 375 | 5 |
| 200 | 400 | 6 |
| 220 | 425 | 7 |
| 230 | 450 | 8 |
| 240 | 475 | 9 |

The following equivalents were used in converting between metric and imperial measurements.

## Volume

| Vol ml/L | Vol Pt/ fl oz |
|----------|---------------|
| 3.40L | 6pt |
| 2.75L | 5pt |
| 2.25L | 4pt |
| 1.70L | 3pt |
| 1.40L | $2\frac{1}{2}$pt |
| 1.10L | 2pt |
| 850ml | $1\frac{1}{2}$pt |
| 570ml | 1pt |
| 425ml | $\frac{3}{4}$pt |
| 380ml | $\frac{2}{3}$pt |
| 280ml | $\frac{1}{2}$pt |
| 200ml | 7fl oz |
| 170ml | 6fl oz |
| 140ml | $\frac{1}{4}$pt |
| 115ml | 4 fl oz |
| 70ml | $\frac{1}{8}$pt |

## Weight

| Weight Kg | Weight lb |
|-----------|-----------|
| 1.35kg | 3lb |
| 900g | 2lb |
| 680g | $1\frac{1}{2}$lb |
| 450g | 1lb |
| 400g | 14oz |
| 340g | 12oz |
| 285g | 10oz |
| 225g | 8oz |
| 200g | 7oz |
| 170g | 6oz |
| 140g | 5oz |
| 115g | 4oz |
| 85g | 3oz |
| 70g | $2\frac{1}{2}$oz |
| 55g | 2oz |
| 45g | $1\frac{1}{2}$oz |
| 30g | 1oz |
| 15g | $\frac{1}{2}$oz |

# A Magical Time
# of the Year

H ave you noticed how

every year Christmas

seems to come earlier

and earlier, and the demands that come with

it are greater? But for me it's the most

magical time of the year.

# A Few
## Special Ingredients

### CRANBERRY

This bitter little berry with a sour tart taste is the one we associate with Christmas. Cranberries can be cooked with orange juice and a little sugar to give a tangy taste, mixed with red onions to make a tasty relish, chopped and combined with breadcrumbs and red onions for a stuffing or combined with walnuts and orange peel to make tasty tangy muffins. Combined with other berries they can be poached to make a winter fruit compote. Whichever way you cook them their tartness adds a unique flavour to many dishes.

### GROUND ALMONDS

This is one of the nuts we use throughout the year but especially in festive cookery. In its ground form it has a shortening effect on pastry, and makes a topping for fruit cakes when combined with icing and caster sugar. Almonds are rich in protein, vitamin B and minerals magnesium, potassium and iron.

Nuts store longer in their shells and are best stored in a cool, dry place. Nuts contain oil or fat and will turn rancid over time.

Almonds can today be found in many forms: whole in shells or skins, blanched, sliced, nibbed, flaked, ground or in a paste.

### CINNAMON

This is my favourite sweet spice, available in whole sticks, powdered or in flakes. It has a sweet, hot and spicy flavour and comes from the bark of the cassia tree. Cinnamon has so many uses: you can use it to spice up cakes and muffins, in fruit pies, in mulled wine or punch recipes or liven up winter carrots by cooking with a hint of cinnamon and orange juice, or dust over the top of winter squash. This is the spice I like to mix with icing sugar to dredge over Madeira cakes or muffins.

### ALL-SPICE BERRIES

These little berries are slightly larger than peppercorns and smaller than juniper berries. They can be bought in ground form, although the roughly crushed berries add texture as well as flavour to many dishes. This spice lives up to its name, as it tastes of nutmeg, cloves and cinnamon, and can be used in both sweet and savoury dishes, e.g. to spice cakes, apple pies, pâtés, ketchup, pickles and salsas.

# A Christmas Casserole

A casserole has to be the answer to Christmas entertaining, and this one has many of the flavours of Christmas used in the marinade. Even better it works a treat with pork, chicken or turkey pieces. This casserole is packed with colour, flavour and texture. It is a variation on a Moroccan meat dish, a sophisticated stew called *tagine*.

### DRIED FRUITS
*450g/1lb dried apples, pears, peaches, apricots etc.*
*$^1/_2$ tsp cinnamon powder*
*140ml/$^1/_4$pt orange juice*
*2dssp oil*

### MARINADE
*2 cinnamon sticks*
*5–6 all spice berries*
*rind and juice of clementine orange*
*2dssp runny honey*
*70ml/$^1/_8$pt ruby port*

*900g/2lb pork pieces*
*450g/1lb small onions*
*280ml/$^1/_2$pt vegetable stock*
*140ml/$^1/_4$pt orange juice*
*1dssp oil*

### TO THICKEN
*2dssp orange marmalade or honey*
*or*
*1dssp blended cornflower*

*Serves 8*

Make the marinade by mixing together in a bowl, the cracked cinnamon sticks, crushed all spice berries, orange rind and juice, honey and port. Stir well together then add the pork cut into 1" cubes. Toss around then cover with clingfilm and leave to marinate – the longer the better, and if possible for at least 24 hours.

In a large pan heat the oil, add the onions and cook until lightly golden. Drain the pork pieces and cook along with the onions until golden and well coated. Add the remainder of the marinade, the stock, orange juices, stir well then cook slowly, either on the hob or in the oven at gas mark 3/160°C/325°F for 1–1$^1/_2$ hours until the flavours have concentrated and the pork is almost cooked and tender. In a separate bowl steep the dried fruits in port, orange juice and a hint of cinnamon. Leave for 10–15 minutes before adding to the casserole. Thicken with either blended cornflower, honey or orange marmalade and allow to cook for a further 5 minutes. Serve this party-style dish with flavoured rice, pasta, potatoes or noodles.

*Overleaf: Christmas Casserole and Flavoured Rice*

# Roasted Red Potatoes
# & Onions with Celeriac

A quick way to cook the Christmas vegetables in the oven after the turkey comes out. Celeriac is a vegetable found at Christmas time. Don't be put off by its ugly appearance, as the flavour is excellent.

*3–4 red skinned potatoes*
*1 celeriac, peeled, cut into chunks*
*3–4 red onions, cut into slices*
*2dssp olive oil*
*2dssp balsamic vinegar*
*salt and pepper*

*Serves 4*

Lightly steam the potatoes and peel celeriac then transfer to a roasting dish with the red onions. Pour over the warmed olive oil, balsamic vinegar, salt and pepper then roast in a hot oven, gas mark 6/200°C/400°F for 20–25 minutes until caramelised and golden. Serve at once.

# Braised Bacon-Flavoured Sprouts
# with Ribbon Leeks

I am of the firm belief that vegetables for Christmas should be very tasty and require little effort in cooking. This is why I have combined the sprouts and leeks then braised them in the oven, a great way to concentrate the flavour.

*450g/1lb Brussels sprouts*
*3 leeks, cut into strips*
*140ml/¹/4pt chicken stock*
*2 rashers of bacon, grilled and cut into strips*
*1dssp pine nuts*
*salt and pepper*

*Serves 4–6*

Lightly steam the Brussels sprouts and leeks for several minutes then transfer to an ovenproof dish. Pour over the stock, sprinkle with bacon, pine nuts and seasoning. Cover with foil and braise in the oven at gas mark 5/190°C/375°F for approximately 15 minutes.

# Roasted Turkey Breast with a Cream Cheese & Parsnip Stuffing

If you enjoy eating turkey for Christmas but not every day thereafter, then turkey breast with a cream cheese stuffing is the answer. If you are cooking Christmas dinner for smaller numbers then this might just be the way to do it.

STUFFING
*115g/4oz cream cheese*
*1 carrot, grated*
*1 parsnip, grated*
*55g/2oz white breadcrumbs*
*1" root ginger, finely chopped*
*rind of half an orange*
*1dssp coriander seeds, crushed*
*1 turkey breast 3–4lb/1.5kg approximately*

TO BASTE
*1dssp oil*

TO GLAZE
*30g/1oz butter*
*juice of 2 oranges*
*70g/2oz soft brown sugar*

*Serves 3–4*

Make the stuffing by mixing together the softened cream cheese, grated carrot, parsnip, breadcrumbs, chopped ginger, orange rind and crushed coriander seeds. The combination of grated carrot and parsnip gives this stuffing a better colour, as carrot can be quite intense in colour when cooked. Mix well until the stuffing blends together.

To stuff the turkey breast, loosen the skin gently from the turkey but keep it intact around the edges. Pack the stuffing down well under the skin. Bring the skin back into position. Secure carefully with skewers and transfer to a full lined dish then pour oil over the cleaned skin. To give the turkey a golden glaze, brush with orange juice and brown sugar bubbled together until thick and syrupy.

Cook in the oven at gas mark 5/190°C/375°F for half an hour, then reduce temperature to gas mark 3/160°C/325°F for approximately 1½ hours.

*Overleaf: Roasted Turkey Breast with Roasted Red Potatoes & Onions with Celeriac*

# Cranberry & Tangerine Orange Sauce

This sauce is simple to make, using either fresh or frozen berries. The best of the flavours of Christmas come together in the sauce, the tangy tangerine orange and the bitter cranberry. The colours and flavours are wonderful.

*4dssp concentrated turkey juices*
*115g/4oz cranberries*
*140ml/¹/4pt tangerine orange juice*
*55g/2oz demerara sugar*

*Serves 4–6*

Reduce and concentrate the turkey juices by bubbling for several minutes. Add the cranberries, orange juice and demerara sugar and cook together for 6–8 minutes until thick and the cranberries have popped. Serve hot.

You may want to sweeten the sauce even more and spice it up with a hint of cinnamon. Use either a cinnamon stick bubbled with the sauce or ¹/4 tsp ground cinnamon powder.

# Apricot & Brandy Sauce

Here is a sauce with a bit of a kick. Brandy and apricots work a treat for flavour and the apricot jam used as a thickener keeps the bright vivid colour of the sauce.

*4dssp concentrated turkey juices*
*140ml/¹/4pt vegetable stock*
*55g/2oz apricots, shredded*
*peel of an orange*
*1dssp apricot jam*
*2dssp brandy*

*Serves 4–6*

Drain and strain the turkey juices into a saucepan at a moderate heat, and reduce the liquid to half, concentrating the flavour. Add the stock, shredded apricots, orange peel and apricot jam. Bubble for several minutes until the sauce thickens. Turn off the heat and add the brandy before serving. If you like you can brush the whole turkey with a little of the sauce before serving to bring up the colour and sweeten the flavour of the juices from the turkey.

# All American Spiced Turkey with a Fruit & Nut Stuffing

One of the best ways to bring a new flavour to the Christmas turkey is with the stuffing. In this one I have brought out the flavour of fruit and nuts and spice with the tangy all spice berry. I have used breadcrumbs as the basis of this stuffing, but if you prefer the interesting texture of couscous, this works equally well. It may require a little extra egg to bind it together.

*8–10lb turkey*

*STUFFING*
*170–225g/6–8oz white breadcrumbs*
*55g/2oz dried apricots*
*55g/2oz golden sultanas*
*2tbsp sherry*
*2–3dssp olive oil*
*1 onion, finely chopped*
*4–6 all spice berries, crushed*
*1tsp cinnamon powder*
*55g/2oz brazil nuts*
*juice of tangerine orange*
*1 egg*
*parsley*
*1 onion*

*TO COAT TURKEY*
*4dssp olive oil*
*8–10 all spice berries, crushed*

*TO COOK*
*280ml/¹/2pt stock*

*FINAL COATING*
*140ml/¹/4pt honey*
*6–8 all spice berries, crushed*

*Serves 10*

Prepare the turkey by defrosting completely, then wipe both inside and out before stuffing. I find it best to stuff the neck cavity, allowing air to freely circulate throughout the bird, ensuring even and complete cooking.

To make the stuffing – prepare the breadcrumbs, steep the dried apricots and sultanas in sherry to allow them to soften a little. Heat the oil in a pan and fry the onion until opaque, but do not let the onions become brown. To this add all the other ingredients, the breadcrumbs, steeped fruit, spices, nuts, orange juice and egg to bind. This stuffing may need salt and pepper. Mix well together, then use to stuff the neck cavity. Fold the flap over then pack down well. Into the body cavity place a bunch of parsley and an onion to create flavour and moistness during cooking.

Transfer the stuffed turkey on to foil. Sprinkle olive oil over the bird to help keep it moist during cooking, then scatter the crushed all spice berries over as well. Pour ¹/₂ pt stock around but not over the bird; this will create moisture when the turkey is cooking.

Fold over the foil and cook in the oven at a higher temperature, gas mark 6/220°C/ 425°F for 30 minutes, then reduce to gas mark 3–4/170°C/340°F approximately, to allow the turkey to cook slowly. For an 8lb turkey the cooking time will be 2¹/₂–3 hours, but always check to ensure that the juices are running free and clear, by inserting a skewer into the leg.

Approximately ³/₄ hour before the turkey is cooked, re-open the foil, pour over the warmed honey and crushed all spice berries to allow the turkey to crisp up and become golden. When ready, remove from the oven, fold over the foil and allow to stand. This will give the juices the chance to flow back into the turkey and become more moist.

# Snow Dredged Christmas Muffins

In the weeks before Christmas when time becomes more precious by the minute, there are occasions when the thought of making and rolling out pastry becomes just too much. Well, if you like the spicy flavour of mince pies for the Christmas caller, then use the mincemeat and nuts to make muffins instead.

*225g/8oz mincemeat (approx 4–6dssp)*
*2–3dssp brandy*
*rind of an orange*
*170g/6oz self-raising flour*
*¹/₂ tsp mixed spice*
*¹/₄ tsp salt*
*55g/2oz soft brown sugar*
*85g/3oz softened butter*
*1 egg, lightly beaten*
*4 fl oz milk*
*30g/1oz nuts*
*30g/1oz demerara sugar*

TO DECORATE
*55g/2oz icing sugar*
*1tsp cinnamon powder*

*Makes 12 large or 24 small muffins*

Add a touch of extra flavour to the mincemeat by mixing in the brandy and orange peel. Leave to sit while you make the basic mixture.

Sieve the flour, mixed spice and salt into a bowl and then add the soft brown sugar. Next, in with the mincemeat and the butter slightly softened, either in a microwave or by beating. Mix lightly and add the lightly beaten egg and milk, mixing as little as possible otherwise the muffins will become hard on top. When the mixture is soft enough to drop off the edge of a spoon, then transfer to lined cases inside the muffin tin.

Sprinkle the top of the muffins with chopped nuts and demerara sugar, then bake in the oven at gas mark 5/190°C/375°F for 15 minutes. When cooked, dust with icing sugar and cinnamon mixed together.

# *Christmas Tart*

If you are looking for a very achievable yet stunning pie, then this is the one for Christmas. Made with an easy blender pastry, filled with a crème fraîche and mascarpone cheese, flavoured with cranberries and topped with berries mulled in wine and cinnamon. A truly stunning and delicious pudding for any time of the year but especially Christmas.

*285g/10oz plain flour*
*55g/2oz ground almonds*
*30g/1oz icing sugar*
*rind of half a lemon or lime*
*1 egg yolk, lightly beaten*
*170g/6oz butter, softened*
*2–3dssp milk*

FILLING
*115g/4oz cranberries*
*55g/2oz icing sugar*
*140ml/¼pt water*
*225g/½lb crème fraîche*
*225g/½lb mascarpone cheese*

TOPPING
*450g/1lb packet assorted frozen berried fruits*

MULLED SYRUP
*140ml/¼pt red wine*
*115g/4oz demerara sugar*
*2 cinnamon sticks*

TO DECORATE
*fresh mint leaves*
*55g/2oz icing sugar*

*Serves 10–12*

This is a simple and quick pastry made in the blender and one which is light and crumbly. Into the blender add the flour, ground almonds, icing sugar, lemon rind, lightly beaten egg yolk, softened butter and milk. Mix together until it forms a soft dough.

Wrap in clingfilm and relax in the fridge for 30 minutes before using.

Use $^2/_3$ of the pastry to line a plate 10–12" in diameter, and the remainder to make leaves and berries to decorate the edge. Brush with egg and bake in the oven at gas mark 5/180°C/350°F for 15–20 minutes.

To make the filling, poach the cranberries in the water and icing sugar for 6–7 minutes then leave to cool.

In a separate bowl mix together the crème fraîche and mascarpone cheese, then fold in the cooked, cooled cranberries and spread over the top of the cooked pastry case.

To prepare the fruits, prepare the mull by heating in a saucepan the red wine, demerara sugar and cinnamon sticks until bubbling then allow them to cool slightly before adding the defrosted fruits. Heat through only for 1–2 minutes then cool. Remove the cinnamon sticks and blend $^1/_4$ of the fruits in a blender and then return to the fruits. This is the best way to thicken them without losing the colour.

Pile high on top of the pie, decorate with mint and dust slightly with icing sugar.

# The Foods from Down Under

**B**arbecues, Pavlovas, Kiwi fruit, Mangoes, Lamb and Lime; now that's the food from Down Under, and you know, Australia is a country whose style and way of doing things has been influenced by just about every cuisine in the world.

# A Few
# Special Ingredients

## SQUASH

Pumpkin and Butternut Squash are probably the two with which we are most familiar, yet they come in many colours and shapes, from summer and winter squashes, marrows, courgettes, to the more unusual custard marrow.

The summer squash can be eaten with the skin, raw, sliced into salads, or cooked by baking, steamed or sautéed e.g. chayote, pallypan, zucchini or yellow squash. The winter varieties e.g. acorn, pumpkin, butternut or spaghetti are cooked and can be flavoured with orange juice, basil, black pepper, chives, onion, mint or parsley.

Whatever the season, buy squash that are firm with no cracks, and store in a cool, well–ventilated, dry place. They should not be stored in a refrigerator, as they may soften. There are approximately 25 calories per 100g.

## KIWI FRUIT

This fruit which looks like a fuzzy brown egg, originated from China, hence its other name, the Chinese gooseberry. Yet, most of our imports of this fruit come to us from New Zealand. It got its name from the country's native bird, the Kiwi. The bright green flesh, studded with tiny, black edible seeds, is packed full of vitamin C. Kiwi fruit can be eaten by cutting in half and scooping out the flesh with a spoon or peeling the fruit and cutting into slices or wedges. There are enzymes in the fruit which help to tenderise meat and chicken, so it works well in a marinade. They are also ideal used as a garnish on their own, in sorbets, ices or fruit salads and, even better, they don't bruise easily during preparation. The skin is edible, but not the most delicious food I've tasted due to its texture and coarseness.

## GREEN SHELLED MUSSELS

Often referred to as the exotic green shelled mussel, they are now being imported from New Zealand. This mussel does not taste particularly different from the blue mussel with which we are more familiar. The flesh of both can vary from ivory, to ivory edged with deep orange or black. It is important to buy them fresh, and to avoid any with cracked shells. However, I find them easier to come by frozen.

## MACADAMIA NUT

This is quite a large, round nut, light brown in colour. It is very difficult to remove from the shell, hence one of the reasons for its expense. It is a creamy, buttery, sweet flavoured nut and, as with any nut, toasting or roasting will bring out its flavour and aroma. To roast, spread the whole shelled nuts on a baking sheet in a baking tin at gas mark 4/ 180°C/350°F for 5–6 minutes, shaking the tin every so often, as this will intensify the flavour. Like almonds under a grill, keep your eye on them, as they can toast in a flash.

Macadamias are a tropical nut, native to Australia, growing as far south as Sydney. Nuts contain oils which are high in vitamin C, as well as being high in fat.

# A Down Under Meringue with Kiwi Fruit & Strawberry

Probably Australia's most popular dessert is the pavlova, created for the famous ballet dancer Anna Pavlova, who came to Australia over 60 years ago. In this recipe I have used the basic pavlova ingredients, but cooked it in a different shape – a roulade – and rolled up the meringue. Use more cream if liked for the filling.

*4 egg whites*
*225g/8oz caster sugar*
*1tsp corn flour*
*1tsp white vinegar*
*few drops vanilla essence*
*55g/2oz chopped nuts*

### FILLING
*2 kiwi fruit*
*280ml/¹/₂pt whipped cream, yoghurt or crème fraîche*

### TO DECORATE
*450g/1lb assorted fruits e.g. kiwi, raspberry, strawberry,*
*passion fruit, peach, or any seasonal fruits*

*Serves 8*

Separate the egg whites from the yolks. Beat the whites together with half the caster sugar until stiff and forming peaks (approximately 5 minutes of beating). Fold in the remainder of the sugar, mixing gently. Add the corn flour, vinegar, vanilla essence and chopped nuts, mixing lightly before transferring to a lined Swiss Roll tin.

To prepare the tin (approximately 9" x 13" x 1") cut a piece of greaseproof paper roughly 2" larger than the tin. Grease the paper on the underside, snipping the corners of the paper to ensure an even shape. Transfer the meringue to the tin, flatten and bake in the oven at gas mark 2/150°C/300°F for 45–50 minutes. When cooked, remove from the oven and cover with a damp tea towel and leave to cool. Then turn out on to a tea towel or greaseproof paper.

To prepare the filling, mix together the chopped kiwi fruit with the cream, yoghurt or crème fraîche. Ensure the meringue is completely cold before spreading with the filling. Spread ²/₃ over the top of the flat meringue and then roll up. Then use the remainder to spread over the outside and decorate with fresh fruit.

*Overleaf: Down Under Meringue*

# Baby Potatoes with Mint & Spring Onions

A simple treatment of smaller potatoes, where they are oven-baked and flavoured with herbs.

*900g/2lb baby potatoes, lightly steamed*
*280ml/¹/₂pt cream, or cream and milk mixed*
*1dssp spring onions*
*1dssp mint, finely chopped*

*Serves 4*

Lightly steam the potatoes for 5–6 minutes, then transfer to a lightly greased ovenproof dish. Pour over the cream, spring onions and mint, and bake in a preheated oven, gas mark 6/200°C/400°F for 15 minutes until well cooked.

Steaming is not essential, but it will shorten the cooking time in the oven, and therefore improve the flavour of the dish.

# Caramelised Onion

Any type of onion can be used for this dish. If using the larger onion, cut into chunks: slow cooking will weaken the flavour, if that's the way you prefer them.

*30g/1oz butter or polyunsaturated fat*
*55g/2oz demerara sugar*
*450g/1lb baby onions*
*2–3dssp balsamic vinegar*

*Serves 4*

Melt the butter and sugar in a pan, then toss in the onions. Stir until well coated, then pour over the balsamic vinegar. Cook for 10 minutes in the pan, then transfer to an ovenproof dish, cooking at gas mark 6/200°C/400°F for 15–20 minutes. The cooking time will sweeten the flavour and lose the strength of the onion. Serve hot.

# Stir Fry of Scallops, Prawns, Green Lip Mussels & Oyster Mushrooms

Stir frying is one of the quickest and best ways to prepare fish, as it retains the fullness of flavour, due to the short cooking time. The flavours of the Orient and Mediterranean come together in this dish, combining the best of prawns, scallops and mussels.

*450g/1lb green lip mussels*
*1dssp olive oil*
*1" root ginger, peeled and chopped*
*450g/1lb scallops*
*450g/1lb prawns*

MARINADE
*1 egg white, lightly beaten*
*15g/¹/₂oz corn flour*
*6 spring onions, cut into strips*
*1 red pepper, finely diced*
*2dssp lemon juice*
*1dssp soy sauce*
*salt and pepper*
*225g/8oz oyster mushrooms*

PASTA
*2.2L/4pt boiling water*
*1dssp olive oil*
*pinch salt*
*450g/1lb dried green pasta*

TO SERVE
*1dssp parsley, finely chopped*

*Serves 6*

If using fresh prawns in the recipe, cook in boiling water for 6 minutes, then cool and shell. If using fresh scallops, open the shells, rinse well and remove the white part only for this dish. Lightly steam the mussels for 3–4 minutes until lightly cooked.

In a wok, heat the olive oil and fry the ginger for 1 minute. Add the scallops, tossed in a marinade of lightly beaten egg white and corn flour, but drain off the excess before cooking. Cook for 1 minute on a high heat, then add the prawns and toss around. In quick succession add the sliced spring onions, diced pepper, lemon juice, soy sauce and seasoning. Add the mushrooms and heat thoroughly. Serve garnished with parsley.

To cook the pasta, bring 4pt of water to the boil, add 1dssp olive oil and a little salt. Add the dried pasta and cook for 6–7 minutes until tender, then drain. While still warm, toss with a little oil and fresh herbs. Serve hot.

*Overleaf: Stir Fry of Scallops, Prawns, Green Lip Mussels & Oyster Mushrooms*

# Damper

Damper is the traditional name for an Australian bread. It is a very tasty bread which can be made either in a tin, or shaped into a flat round bread and cooked on a baking sheet. I prefer the flatter shape, as the bread cooks more easily. If you prefer, it can be made and cooked 1–2" thick.

*450g/1lb soda bread self–raising flour*
*2dssp spring onion, finely chopped*
*2dssp parsley, finely chopped*
*1 onion, finely chopped*
*55g/2oz cheddar cheese, grated*
*salt and pepper*
*280ml/¹⁄2pt milk and water, mixed*

*Serves 6*

Sieve the flour into a bowl and add the chopped spring onion, parsley, onion, grated cheese and seasoning. Mix well, then add the mixed milk and water, and combine until it forms a soft dough. Knead lightly, then shape into a flat round, and place on a floured baking sheet. Bake in the oven for 20–25 minutes at gas mark 6/200°C/400°F.

# Puréed Squash

Squash vary greatly with the season, but treat them all in exactly the same way and use them as an alternative to turnips in recipes.

*1 butternut squash, steamed*
*1 gem squash, steamed*
*pinch nutmeg*
*pinch paprika*
*2dssp orange juice*

*Serves 4*

Peel and dice the squash and remove any seeds. I find steaming the best way to cook squash or pumpkin. Cook for 20 minutes until tender. Mash and add nutmeg, paprika and orange juice. Serve warm.

# Baked Lamb Chops
# with a Barbecue Sauce

Lamb is very popular in Australia and New Zealand, as well as here at home, whether you are roasting a leg, cooking a crown or making a stew. This dish of tender leg chops cooked in a barbecue sauce is robust, tasty and easily cooked.

*30g/1oz butter*
*1dssp oil*
*3 cloves garlic, coarsely chopped*
*2 onions*
*55g/2oz soft brown sugar*
*4 x 225–340g/8–12oz tender lamb leg chops*
*1dssp chilli paste*
*440g/2 large cans chopped tomatoes*
*2dssp soy sauce*
*small bunch rosemary*
*280ml/$^1$/2pt vegetable stock*
*salt and pepper*

To serve
*parsley, finely chopped*

*Serves 4*

Heat the butter and oil together in a pan, when hot, add the garlic and onion. Cook until it begins to caramelise, then add the brown sugar and cook until the onions are well coated. Add the chops to the hot pan and coat well on either side for at least 6 minutes until golden and the juices are well sealed in. This initial cooking will be important to the final colour of this dish.

Add the ingredients for the barbecue sauce; chilli paste for heat, chopped tomatoes for colour and flavour, soy sauce for flavour, and rosemary to bring out the wild woody flavour. Add the stock and seasoning, place the lid on top and transfer to the oven. Bake at gas mark 5/190°C/375°F for at least 30 minutes. If preferred, this dish can also be cooked on top of the hob and simmered slowly for a similar length of time.

Serve hot with chopped parsley and potatoes or damper bread and squash.

*Overleaf: Baked Lamb Chops with Damper and Puréed Squash*

# Kiwi Lime & Coconut Chicken

Kiwi fruit, or Chinese gooseberries as they are sometimes called, are packed full of flavour, colour and sweetness. This chicken dish uses kiwi both in the marinade and the sauce. It is a dish which does not hold for long, as the vivid green colour of the kiwi will spoil on over cooking.

*4 chicken fillets, cut into strips*

### MARINADE
*1dssp sherry vinegar*
*1dssp lime juice*
*2–3 kiwi fruit*

### TO COOK
*1oz butter*
*1dssp olive oil*
*1dssp honey*

### SAUCE
*140ml/¹/₄pt canned coconut milk*
*70ml/¹/₈pt cream*
*2 kiwi fruits, diced*
*1dssp spring onions*
*salt and pepper*
*peel of a lime, finely grated*

### TO GARNISH
*1dssp parsley, finely chopped*

*Serves 4*

Cut the chicken fillets into good sized strips approximately ¹/₂" thick and 3" long. Prepare the marinade by mixing together the diced kiwi fruit, sherry vinegar, lime juice and seasoning. Add the chicken strips, stir well and leave to marinate for 30 minutes.

To cook the chicken, melt the butter in a pan, add the olive oil and honey and, when bubbling, add the chicken. The honey will sweeten the chicken during cooking, but be careful not to overcook. Toss for 2–3 minutes on either side until almost cooked and the liquid in the pan reduced.

Add the coconut milk and, if liked, a little cream. Add the diced kiwi fruit, spring onions, salt and pepper and lime peel. Simmer gently for 5–6 minutes over a low heat until the chicken is cooked through. Cooking time will vary with the thickness of the cooked chicken fillets, but test just before serving. Garnish with finely chopped parsley.

# A Peach & Paw Paw Pudding

Peaches and Paw Paw, or Papaya, can both be found in Australia and here at home. These two fruits combine well together under a light creamy crust of cinnamon flavoured custard.

*3 paw paw*
*juice of a lime*
*3 peaches*
*1 packet 20 sponge fingers*
*2–3dssp peach liqueur*

SAUCE
*3 egg yolks*
*85g/3oz caster sugar*
*2dssp white wine*
*70ml/¹/₈pt cream (optional)*

TOPPING
*55g/2oz icing sugar*
*¹/₂ tsp cinnamon powder*

TO SERVE
*55g/2oz toasted flaked almonds*
*Sprig of mint*

*Serves 4–6*

Prepare the paw paw by cutting in half, remove the black seeds from the centre, then peel and cut into fine slices. Place in a bowl and sprinkle with lime juice to develop the acidity and bring out the flavour of strawberries, melons and peaches combined together. Cut the peaches into slices and mix with the paw paw. Arrange the sponge fingers on an ovenproof serving dish and sprinkle with the peach liqueur. Pour the fruits over the top of the sponge finger and leave to sit for several minutes while the sauce is made. The fruit juice will also flavour the sponge fingers and soften them.

To make the sauce, whisk the egg yolks and caster sugar together for 5–6 minutes over warm water until cooked, light, white and fluffy. Add the wine. If liked, 70ml/¹/₈pt cream can be added to this sauce. Pour over the fruit and sponge fingers and dust with icing sugar and cinnamon mixed together. Flash below a very hot grill for 1–2 minutes and serve hot, sprinkled with toasted flaked almonds and a sprig of mint.

# Savouring Spain

I f I was to say Bitter Seville

Oranges, Sherry Olives, oil and

onions then I'm talking about the

sun-drenched food of the sun, and we're

Savouring Spain.

# A Few
# Special Ingredients

### Spanish Olive Oil

Many varieties of these oils are available, e.g. Spanish extra virgin olive oil, which comes from the very finest of olives. Although the most expensive, its flavour is excellent and is best used as a condiment poured over hot dishes and salads to bring out the best of its flavour. I feel it's a waste to cook with this type of oil, preferring to use it unheated for the finest result.

The Spanish virgin olive oil can be used for both cooking and in salad dressings. As a rule not as expensive as the extra virgin olive oil. Like so many oils the flavour will depend on the variety and ripeness of the olives used. The versatile Spanish olive oil is a blend of refined olive oil and virgin olive oil and much cheaper. This can be used for cooking, in salads and even in baking a healthy olive oil loaf or cake.

All olive oils with monosaturated fat are healthier in the diet and olives themselves, whether the tasty green or the riper black variety are rich in vitamin A, potassium, phosphorus or magnesium, and if it's calories you are concerned about a 4oz quantity of olive oil contains only 40 calories.

### Peppers

Peppers are a member of the capsicum family and it is the Spanish who lay claim to having brought them to Europe from Central America.

This colourful vegetable is very popular in Spanish cooking. Many varieties can be bought dried, and jars or cans of skinned peppers called pimentos are now widely available. Canned peppers can be substituted in recipes requiring fresh peppers.

They store well and have a good shelf life but are best kept in a cold, dark place or in the refrigerator. Like most vegetables, remove any plastic wrapping before storage as this leads to condensation causing vegetables to deteriorate more easily.

Cook them by stir frying, oven roasting, steaming, poaching in syrup or even in the microwave.

### Chorizo Sausage

This rusty red sausage aromatic with red pepper is used widely throughout Spain, but we too are using this flavoursome sausage more and more. It needs no preparation, is full of flavour and makes an ideal fast food with many possibilities, good in a tasty omelette, as a topping for pizzas or ideal just on its own with salads or in a sandwich.

### Seville Oranges

When buying oranges, the skin is a good indication of quality. If the orange is heavy for its size this indicates one packed full of juice – don't always go for the largest. A tip to extract the maximum amount of juice is to warm the orange for 25–30 seconds in the microwave or roll it in your hands for a few seconds.

Seville oranges are used widely in the making of marmalade due to their bitter flesh which gives a sharp tangy taste. They are excellent when used to complement rich meats or simply for a tangy, sharp orange sauce.

# A Mediterranean
# Stuffed Pork Fillet

Pork fillet stuffed with breadcrumbs is probably our most popular way of cooking it. But here's a Mediterranean version where the pork is stuffed with golden grained couscous, apricots and sultanas soaked in Spanish sherry, then roasted in the oven. The flavour of the apricots is used again in the sauce.

*2 pork fillets, approximately 680g/1¹/₂lb each in weight*
*1dssp sherry*
*15g/¹/₂oz demerara sugar*
*280ml/¹/₂pt boiling water*
*115–170g/4–6oz couscous*
*115g/4oz dried apricots, diced*
*115g/4oz sultanas*
*70ml/¹/₈pt dry sherry*
*15g/¹/₂oz demerara sugar*
*¹/₂ egg, lightly beaten*

To roast
*2dssp olive oil*
*2dssp sherry*
*2dssp honey*
*salt and pepper*

*Serves 6–8*

Prepare the pork fillet by removing any visible fat then slice down the centre and flatten out with a rolling pin until the pork fillet is quite thin. Sprinkle with sherry and ¹/₂ oz demerara sugar.

Pour the boiling water over the couscous and leave for 15–20 minutes until the couscous swells up and almost doubles in size. It will absorb the liquid as it sits.

Mix together the diced apricots and sultanas, pour over the sherry and a sprinkle of demerara sugar. Leave to sit for 15 minutes then mix together with the couscous, chopped parsley and lightly beaten egg. When well mixed, spoon over the pork, flatten down well and roll up from end to end. Secure with string or skewers. Transfer to a foil lined dish, pour over a little oil, marinade of sherry and honey, add salt and pepper and roast in the oven at gas mark 5/180°C/350°F for approximately 1 hour. Again the cooking time will vary with the thickness of the pork but allow at least 1 hour for the pork to be well cooked. If the two are being sandwiched together with the stuffing then cooking time will be approximately 1¹/₂– 1³/₄ hours.

*Overleaf: Mediterranean Stuffed Pork Fillet, Snappy Bean Salad and Couscous Salad*

# Burnt Apricot Sauce

An almost burnt caramelized sauce with pork works well. This time I'm using the canned apricots with their sweeter flavour and combining this flavour with the sherry and the concentrated pork juices.

*140ml/¹/₄pt cooked pork juices, strained*
*60g/2oz demerara sugar*
*70ml/¹/₈pt remainder of sherry marinade*
*1 x 410 g can apricots*

*Serves 4–6*

Strain the pork juices into a pan and mix with the demerara sugar. Stir over a high temperature to almost caramelize the juices. Add the sherry marinade and canned apricots and bubble rapidly until the sauce becomes concentrated, dark golden and the apricots coated. If you prefer a smoother sauce, the apricots can be finely chopped and blended before adding to the sauce.

# Warm Couscous Salad

Couscous, this most versatile grain is excellent in salads where you want a lighter flavour. I have heated the olive oil and garlic and served the salad slightly warm.

*435/³/₄pt boiling water*
*2dssp olive oil*
*2 cloves garlic, finely chopped*
*220g/8oz couscous*
*1 beef tomato, deseeded and diced*
*55g/2oz toasted pine nuts*
*2 spring onions, finely sliced*

To garnish
*basil or parsley, finely chopped*

*Serves 6*

To prepare the couscous, add to the water and leave to infuse for 15 minutes. Heat the oil and garlic together until brown and nutty. Pour this mixture over the prepared couscous.

Add the diced tomato, toasted pine nuts and spring onions mix lightly and serve warm. Garnish with finely chopped herbs such as basil or parsley for a little colour.

# *Flamenco*
# *Soup*

Peppers are one of the most useful ingredients. The colour matches the flavour: bright, yellow peppers are sweet and green peppers are sharper-tasting and more bitter. It's the yellow bell pepper that I'm using in this soup, flavoured with a hint of oregano. Try the same basic recipe but substitute the peppers for beef tomatoes and the oregano for basil and you have another soup simply made which you can serve with the pepper one side by side in the dish.

*6 yellow peppers*
*2 cloves garlic, finely chopped*
*1–2 large Spanish onions*
*1dssp olive oil*
*¹/₂ tsp oregano*
*850ml/1¹/₂pts light vegetable or chicken stock*

To garnish
*swirl of yoghurt*

*Serves 8*

Roast the whole peppers in the oven at gas mark 6/200°C/400°F for approximately 30 minutes. This will soften and sweeten the flavours and make it easier to remove the skin. Cut the peppers into chunks.

In a large heavy based pan gently cook together the garlic, onion and oil, being careful not to let them brown as the colour of the soup is so important. This slow initial cooking should take 6–7 minutes until the onions are softened.

Peel the peppers, cut into chunks and add to the pan. Toss around until coated but again be careful not to let them brown. Add the oregano and stock to the soup. Put the lid on top and leave to simmer for approximately 20 minutes until the vegetables are soft and well blended. Mix in the food processor then return to the pot. Adjust the seasoning and consistency of the soup with the stock. There is no flour used as a thickener in the soup as it would spoil the colour.

Serve hot with a swirl of yoghurt or even a dash of sherry.

*Overleaf: Flamenco Soup*

# Snappy Bean Salad

The simplest of salads which uses the best and freshest of the summer bean crop. However as they have a short season, the beans can be mixed with mangetout peas, peas and spring onions to give a tasty fresh salad. My favourite are the big, flat, green broad beans in this recipe, but remember to shell them from the white coating so they will be brighter green.

*225g/8oz green beans*
*225g/8oz mangetout peas*
*2–3 spring onions*

DRESSING
*3dssp olive oil*
*1dssp honey*
*1dssp sherry*
*salt and pepper*

TO SERVE
*1dssp parsley, finely chopped*

*Serves 4–6*

Lightly steam the beans and mangetout peas. Mix while still warm with the spring onions.
   To prepare the dressing, mix together the hot oil, honey and sherry, add salt and pepper to taste. Pour over the vegetables and serve warm. Garnish with chopped parsley.

# A Spanish Omelette

The Spanish Omelette is probably one of Spain's most popular dishes. Packed full of flavours and open faced, it can be made with onions, garlic, potatoes, peppers and herbs. It is super served either as a meal or a snack. I like to serve it cut into wedges with a bowl of salad.

*6 eggs, lightly whisked*
*salt and pepper*
*1 large Spanish onion, finely chopped*
*2 cloves garlic*
*2dssp olive oil*
*15g/¹/₂oz butter*
*1 red pepper, diced*
*1 yellow pepper, diced*
*225g/8oz potatoes, sliced, lightly steamed*

*225g/8oz ham or bacon, dry cured or cooked*

TO SERVE
*2dssp finely chopped herbs e.g. basil, parsley or chives*

*Serves 4–6*

Beat the eggs lightly in a bowl but do not over beat the eggs. Add salt and pepper.

To prepare the filling, finely chop the onion and garlic then cook in a large pan with a little oil. The size of the dish is important in relation to the quantity of the eggs. Heat the oil and if liked a little butter can be added for flavour – this also helps to stop the omelette sticking to the pan.

Next add the peppers and sliced steamed potatoes and toss around for several minutes. Drain the vegetables and add to the egg mixture and mix lightly. Re-heat the oil in the pan before pouring the omelette mixture back into the pan. Scatter the ham over the top and cook for 2–3 minutes until lightly set. Flash the omelette below a hot grill. This way the omelette cooks more easily and sets lightly puffed up.

Scatter with finely chopped herbs and serve hot with salad.

# *A Bitter Sweet Seville Orange Pudding*

The Seville Orange with its sharp bitter flavour is ideal for this sauce, but as it has such a short season you may use oranges bitter of flavour and full of juice. Combined with the sweetness of the double layered meringue this is one pudding which looks stunning for that special occasion. The secret in any meringue is to use eggs at least one week old and to separate the whites from the yolks carefully.

LAYER 1
*4 egg whites*
*115g/4oz caster sugar*

LAYER 2
*1 egg*
*1 egg yolk*
*30g/1oz caster sugar*
*30g/1oz hazelnuts, ground*
*30g/1oz plain flour*

ORANGE SAUCE
*4 small oranges, sliced and juiced*
*55g/2oz kumquats (optional)*
*55g/2oz butter*
*55g/2oz demerara sugar*
*1dssp Spanish sherry*

*Serves 8–10*

*Overleaf: Bitter Sweet Seville Orange Pudding*

To make the first layer beat the egg whites and half the sugar together until light and fluffy then fold in carefully the remainder of the sugar and transfer to a lightly greased angel cake tin (tin with a hole in the centre).

In a separate bowl prepare the second layer. Beat together the egg, egg yolk and caster sugar until light and creamy then fold in the ground hazelnuts and plain flour. Fold in carefully then transfer on top of the first layer, flattening slightly. Cook in a bain-marie for 1 hour at gas mark 4/180°C/350°F. Unmould when just slightly cool, then decorate with sauce poured over the top and flash below the grill.

NB The tin can be lined with greaseproof paper. This helps the meringue to be released more easily.

### ORANGE SAUCE

Peel and slice four oranges, slice the kumquats also if being used. Heat the butter and demerara sugar until golden and bubbling. Add the oranges, kumquats, juice and sherry and cook for 2–3 minutes.

Arrange the fruit over the top of the pudding and pour a little of the sauce over before flashing under a very hot grill. This will give the pudding a wonderful crusty golden top.

# *Whole Baked Fish*

Whole fish cooks best of all if baked in the oven, wrapped in foil to keep in the flavour. A little wine or lemon will improve the colour and butter will help to develop the flavour during baking. Sea bass, salmon, trout, red mullet can all be cooked this way.

*1 whole fish (1¹/₂–2lb), cleaned and sealed*
*15g/¹/₂oz butter*
*¹/₂ lemon, cut into wedges*
*small bunch of herbs*
*salt and pepper*
*1dssp peppercorns*
*¹/₈pt dry white wine or lemon juice*

*Serves 2*

Ask your fishmonger to clean and scale the fish. Using a sharp knife score the fish diagonally to allow the flavours to reach into the fish.

Place the fish on foil, stuffing with the butter, lemon wedges, bunch of herbs, salt and pepper, and peppercorns. Sprinkle with white wine. Fold over the foil and bake in a hot oven at gas mark 6/200°C/400°F for approximately 8–10 minutes per lb. The fish does not require turning during cooking, and you will find the fish looks better if the foil is opened up in the oven for 5–6 minutes before serving to allow it to crisp up slightly.

# Char Grilled Vegetables

A quick summery way to cook most vegetables. Toss with olive oil and black pepper during cooking. If cooked with a few garlic cloves it will enhance the flavour. Most vegetables are suitable for this style of cooking but choose an assortment that look colourful.

*2 potatoes*
*1 head of fennel*
*2 tomatoes*
*2 courgettes*
*2dssp olive oil*
*black pepper*
*4 cloves garlic*

To GARNISH
*basil, finely chopped*

*Serves 6*

Lightly steam the potatoes and fennel for 5 minutes then place on the hot grill pan. Add the tomatoes and courgettes and cook for several minutes until blackened and cooked. Sprinkle a little oil, pepper and garlic over the vegetables during cooking.

The ripeness of some vegetables will affect the cooking time, so watch them carefully. To make the grilled vegetables look even more attractive sprinkle with finely chopped summer herbs, e.g. basil.

# Roasted Lemon & Herb Sauce

Lemons roasted under the grill become sweeter and the juice flows more freely. This light, tangy sauce allows the delicate flavour of fish to come through.

*3 lemons*
*3dssp olive oil*
*salt and pepper*
*$^1/_2$ tsp herb (fennel or dill) fronds, chopped*

*Serves 6*

Cut the lemons in half and roast under a hot grill for about 8 minutes. Squeeze the juice and mix with the olive oil, salt, pepper and finely chopped fennel or dill. Mix well and serve spooned over fish.

# The
# Mexican Way

---

**T**hink about Mexican food
and the words that spring to
mind are 'hot' and 'spicy'.
And the ingredients, well, they're chillies,
peppers, tacos and beans. But that's only part of
the story, because the Mexican way with food is
fresh, flavoursome and oh so colourful.

# A Few
# Special Ingredients

## TORTILLAS

These flat breads made from corn or wheat flour are to the Mexicans what pancakes are to us. They are served as bread on its own or as the basis of many Mexican dishes. They can be used either flat or in many shapes e.g. tacos are corn tortillas packed with a filling and folded in half.

The tortillas made with wheat flour are known as *burritos* and they can be packed with many savoury fillings e.g. fish, shredded chicken or pork and served with salads, guacamole, hot chilli sauce or grated cheese. The possibilities are endless and they make either a quick snack or a very tasty meal.

## GUACAMOLE

This is a sauce or dip in which the main ingredient is mashed avocado pear. It is usually combined with onion, coriander and tomato with a little garlic added but as with so many traditional recipes, it has acquired a few variations along the way. Avocados tend to discolour easily, and you will find the addition of 1dssp of lemon not only improves the colour but sharpens the flavour. This dip is served with many Mexican dishes but is also good to eat on its own with taco chips.

## TABASCO

This is the name of the sauce which is made with the Tabasco chilli – a small one approximately one inch long with a smooth skin and a thin flesh. This is a particularly hot chilli which can be found either red, yellow or orange, and is the main ingredient in Tabasco sauce.

## CHILLIES

There are hundreds of varieties of fresh chillies and yet we find only a couple of varieties on our greengrocer shelves with only a choice of red or green, fat or thin chillies. However we can easily find chillies in other forms, dried in flakes, as a powder, or as a paste and each one if used carefully can create the required amount of heat and colour.

If using fresh chillies remember the longer the chilli is cooked in a dish the hotter the result. If you want to reduce the heat of the chillies before cooking then the little white seeds on the inside of the chilli should be removed. It is almost impossible to reduce the heat of a dish once the chillies have been added, the only ingredient which helps to reduce it is the addition of a little sugar (caster or granulated).

# *Citrus*
# *Marinaded Chicken*

A light chicken dish with the best of the citrus fruits combined with herbs and chillies to make a refreshing, tangy marinade. This marinade takes a longer than usual time to work. However, the result is delicious and well worth the wait, as it is light, refreshing and healthy. Leave to marinate in fridge.

*1 orange, cut into chunks with skin on*
*1 lemon, cut into chunks with skin on*
*1 lime, cut into chunks with skin on*
*2 cloves garlic*
*2 red chillies*
*1 small bunch/approx 2dssp coriander*
*¹/₂ tsp oregano*
*2dssp honey*
*70mls–140mls/¹/₈–¹/₄pt fruit juice*
*4 chicken fillets, 115g–170g/4–6oz in size*

*Serves 4*

Prepare the marinade in a blender by mixing together the orange, lemon, lime (cut into chunks), two cloves garlic, 2 chillies de-seeded and veins removed, a small bunch coriander, ¹/₂ tsp oregano, 2dssp honey and blend together for 1–2 minutes. If the marinade is a little thick, then it can be thinned down with fruit juice. Pour over the chicken fillets, cover and leave to marinate for 12 hours at least. The flavours of this marinade take some time to work.

To cook, shake a little of the excess marinade off the chicken fillets before cooking on a preheated, lightly oiled grill pan. Cook the fillets for approximately 4 minutes on each side, turning only once. Check to ensure the fillets are cooked well, then serve with rice, potatoes or salad.

*Overleaf: Citrus Marinaded Chicken, New Mexican Rice and Zingy Coleslaw*

# A Zingy
# Colourful Coleslaw

Here's a zingy, colourful coleslaw without a trace of oil or mayonnaise. The combination of lime and honey works well as a dressing but should be used the day it is made.

*1/2 small white cabbage, shredded*
*few leaves red Radicchio lettuce*
*1 small red onion*
*1 small white onion*
*1 yellow pepper, roasted*
*1 orange pepper, roasted*

### DRESSING
*2dssp honey*
*2dssp lime juice*
*1/4 tsp mustard*
*salt and pepper*

*Serves 6–8*

To prepare the vegetables for the coleslaw, slice the cabbage very finely along with the red and white onions. Tear the red lettuce into small pieces and mix with the other ingredients. Prepare the peppers by cutting into strips, removing the seeds and grilling for 2 minutes on either side. This improves and sweetens the flavour of the peppers.

Prepare the dressing, by mixing together the honey, lime juice, salt, pepper and mustard until smooth and well blended. Pour over the salad ingredients, toss well, then serve.

# Spicy Red
# Chilli Sauce

Mexican sauces are hot, spicy and very versatile. This one is ideal to serve with tacos, tortillas, or with a quick snack.

*1 onion*
*2 cloves garlic*
*1dssp oil*
*1 red chilli, chopped*
*1tsp tomato paste*
*1dssp brown sugar*
*1/2 can chopped pimentos*
*1tsp oregano*
*140ml/1/4pt water*

*Serves 6*

Cook the onion and garlic in the oil, then add the chopped chilli, tomato paste, brown sugar and stir well before adding the pimentos, oregano and water. Simmer gently for 10 minutes. Then serve.

# Mexican
# Chocolate Pudding

Here is a chocolate pudding that is rich, dark and bitter and topped with lime and almond. A most interesting combination of flavours with the chocolate and coffee flavoured with cinnamon and vanilla. Serve as a cake or pudding.

### BASE
*4tsp coffee*
*70ml/¹/₈pt hot water*
*55g/2oz ground almonds*
*¹/₂ tsp cinnamon powder*
*few drops vanilla essence*
*70g/2¹/₂oz melted fat (butter or polyunsaturated fat)*
*170g/6oz almond biscuits, crushed*

### FILLING
*340g/12oz cream cheese*
*115g/4oz icing sugar*
*115g/4oz chocolate, melted*
*225g/8oz yoghurt*
*225g/8oz fromage frais*
*3 eggs, lightly beaten*

### TOPPING
*225g/8oz crème fraîche*
*zest of 1 lime*
*55g/2oz flaked almonds, toasted*
*2 amaretto biscuits, crushed*

*Serves 10*

Prepare the coffee mixture by mixing together the strong coffee with the hot water, ground almonds, cinnamon powder and vanilla essence. Prepare the base by melting the butter in a pan, add the crushed biscuits and mix well together. Then transfer to a lightly oiled 7–8" tin – preferably loose bottomed.

Prepare the filling by beating together the cream cheese, icing sugar until light and fluffy and add the coffee mixture and slightly warm melted chocolate. Fold both in together and only mix until both the chocolate and coffee mixture are incorporated. Add the

*Overleaf: Mexican Chocolate Pudding*

yoghurt and fromage frais, folding in between each addition, then finally add the lightly beaten eggs. When the chocolate mixture is smooth, pour over the crushed biscuit base, bake at gas mark 3/160°C/325°F for approximately 1 hour until the cake is firm to the touch and cooked. Leave to cool.

Make the topping by mixing together the crème fraîche with the lime zest, crushed almond flakes and spread over the top of the cake when cold.

Serve decorated with a little fruit and crushed biscuits.

# Ranchero Potatoes

Lightly steamed potato wedges, flavoured with paprika and baked in the oven.

*680g/1½ lb potatoes, cut into wedges*
*1dssp oil*
*1tsp paprika pepper*
*sprinkling of black pepper*

To serve
*1 carton soured cream*
*2dssp chives, chopped*

*Serves 4–6*

Cut the potatoes into good sized wedges, then steam for 6–8 minutes until almost cooked. Transfer on to a baking sheet and when still hot, sprinkle with oil, dust with paprika and pepper, then bake in the oven at gas mark 6/200°C/400°F for 15–20 minutes until the potatoes are softened and golden.

Serve hot with soured cream and finely chopped chives.

# Chile Chilli Con Carne

Chilli Con Carne, that savoury mix of meat, heat and beans started life with the Texan cowboy and spread across the world to become one of our best known dishes. The heat can be easily adjusted with the amount of chilli whether fresh, flakes, powdered or in a paste.

*1dssp oil*
*1 onion, finely chopped*
*680g/1¹/₂1b lean minced steak*
*2 rashers bacon, diced*
*2tsp chilli powder*
*1tsp chilli flakes*
*1tsp oregano*
*1tsp cumin powder*
*pinch of salt*
*400g (1 x 14oz can) chopped tomatoes*
*2dssp tomato purée or paste*
*400g (1 x 14oz can) kidney beans*
*280ml/¹/₂pt stock*
*1tsp sugar*

To serve
*140ml/¹/₄pt yoghurt or soured cream*

*Serves 4–6*

Heat the oil in a pan and fry the onions for several minutes. In batches add the minced steak and cook well over a high heat between each addition. This will seal the flavour well into the meat and improve the colour of the finished dish. Add the diced bacon rashers. Next, add the spices, chilli powder, chilli flakes, dried oregano and finally the cumin powder. Stir and cook the spices for 5 minutes to release their flavour and heat. Add a pinch of salt, can of chopped tomatoes, tomato purée and cook for several minutes. Add the beans, either red kidney or pinto or a combination of both. I am using the canned beans which do not require steeping and are more convenient. Add the stock and a pinch of sugar which helps to regulate the heat of the chilli powder during cooking.

Simmer for 1¹/₂–2 hours, then serve with rice or potatoes. A little soured cream or yoghurt is delicious served on top of the chilli.

*Overleaf: Chile Chilli Con Carne and Ranchero Potatoes*

# A Santa Fe
# Pork Molé

This is an interesting combination of pork with a nutty, spicy hot sauce. Traditional Mexican molé has melted chocolate added to it just before serving, one ingredient which I must admit I have not quite got used to in this dish. So this is my version with a super nutty texture and a hot spicy flavour, but not too hot – only a couple of chillies!

*680g/1¹/₂lb lean pork pieces, cut into chunks*
*4dssp lime juice*
*2dssp light oil*
*2 cloves garlic, peeled but whole*
*115g/4oz pumpkin seeds, unsalted and unroasted*
*55g/2oz whole almonds, shelled*
*1 red chilli, deseeded, veins removed*
*1 green chilli, deseeded, veins removed*
*1 cinnamon stick*
*70ml/¹/₈pt lemon and lime juice*
*1 green pepper, cut into dice*
*400g (1 x 14oz can) chopped tomatoes*
*2dssp tomato purée*
*salt to taste*
*1oz sunflower seeds to garnish*

*Serves 4–6*

To prepare the pork, cut into bitesize pieces and then toss in the lime juice and 1 dssp of oil and leave to marinade for at least ¹/₂ hour while you make the sauce.

To prepare molé, dry roast or place in a grill pan under a medium heat for several minutes to intensify the flavour of the sauce ingredients.

Peel the garlic, shell the whole almonds, deseed the chillies and cut in half, add the pumpkin seeds, then place all of them on the grill pan but be careful not to let them char.

After roasting, transfer to a blender along with 1 cinnamon stick, approximately ¹/₈pt lemon and lime juice and blend to a smooth but soft paste then transfer to a bowl. Adjust the consistency with more lemon juice if needed.

Heat 1 dssp oil in a large pan and cook the pork in batches to keep the temperature high and keep in all the flavour. Add in one diced green pepper and cook for another minute. Next in with the sauce and molé, keeping the temperature high still for 3–4 minutes to evaporate off the liquid and concentrate the flavours. Add the chopped tomatoes, tomato purée and adjust the seasoning with a little salt. Cook for 20–25 minutes.

Garnish with sunflower seeds and serve.

# New Mexican Rice

Rice goes particularly well with most Mexican dishes, but the rice can easily be spiced up to your taste.

*1dssp oil*
*2 cloves garlic*
*1 small onion, finely diced*
*225g/8oz patna long grain rice*
*280–420ml/¹/₂–³/₄pt vegetable stock*
*1dssp tomato paste*
*1 tomato, diced & de-seeded*

TO SERVE
*fresh parsley or coriander*

*Serves 3–4*

In a large pan fry together the oil, garlic and onion until lightly cooked and almost opaque. Add the washed and dried long grain rice and stir around until all the grains become well coated. Add the stock, stir several times, then leave to simmer gently for 8–10 minutes until the rice has absorbed the liquid. Stir the rice, only slightly, and add the tomato paste and diced tomato. Mix and serve hot garnished with parsley or coriander.

# The Glorious Food of Greece

B aklava, moussaka and velvet textured desserts are only some of the sumptuous foods to come from Greece. Aubergines, tzatziki and eating under sun-drenched vines are pleasures also enjoyed in Greece, which make the food of Greece quite an experience.

# A Few
## Special Ingredients

### TARAMASALATA

Fish roe is the main ingredient in this popular snack. Fresh or dried roe from either cod or grey mullet is used. The fish roe, stale breadcrumbs, lemon juice and onion are combined in a blender and olive oil is added to adjust the consistency. The texture resembles a fine pâté and can be served with fresh olives.

### HALLOUMI

Another sheep's cheese, perhaps not as well known as Feta, but widely used in Greek cookery. Quite a firm cheese, it is often cut into slices, brushed with olive oil and grilled.

### MEZZE

A style of eating that originated in the tavernas of Greece and has now spread throughout the world. A casual affair, with bowls of tzatziki, olives, pitta bread and salads. In fact, foods that exemplify the relaxed way of eating throughout Greece.

# Harvest Time Chicken

This is a very old recipe based on the Greek way with walnuts cooked in a sauce. Chicken is so popular in our diet that it is always good to find new ways to cook it, and sauces to combine with it. Char grilling chicken has become very popular and this nutty flavoured sauce works a treat with char grilled chicken. Many different nuts combine with the flavour of chicken, but I like this nutty sauce best of all if it is made with the singular flavour of nuts such as hazelnuts, brazil nuts or walnuts. The chicken can be flavoured or spiced with either paprika or cayenne pepper added to the flour.

*4 chicken fillets, whole or cut into strips*
*30g/1oz flour*
*$^1$/2 tsp paprika or cayenne pepper*
*30g/1oz butter*
*2dssp olive oil*

### Nutty Sauce
*55g/2oz ground nuts e.g. hazelnuts, brazil nuts or walnuts*
*30g/1oz whole nuts, coarsely cut*
*70ml/$^1$/8pt white wine*
*280ml/$^1$/2pt vegetable stock*
*$^1$/2 small leek, finely shredded*
*$^1$/2 lemon rind and juice*
*2dssp cream*
*1dssp parsley, finely chopped*

*Serves 4*

Prepare the chicken by cutting the fillets into strips, or leave whole. Toss in flour and spice and cook brushed with oil on the grill, or in oil and butter in the frying pan. Cook until almost tender, and add the remaining ingredients to the frying pan. If the chicken has been cooked in the grill pan, add a little extra oil and butter along with the other ingredients. Add the wine and stock and simmer gently until the chicken is cooked and the liquid has reduced down and become syrupy. Add the ground nuts, shredded leek, lemon rind and juice, cream and parsley. Stir and cook for several minutes until the sauce thickens, then serve. Serve garnished with chopped nuts scattered on top of the chicken.

# Tzatziki

There is no dip in Greece more popular than the tangy, almost bitter tzatziki. Made with their popular Greek yoghurt, the texture is creamy and the flavour sharp, with the addition of mint, vinegar and cucumber. This sauce is popular as a tangy dip. A new popular idea is to deep fry finely sliced vegetables until golden and crispy. Aubergines, parsnips and potatoes are three of my favourite vegetables to serve in this way, with tzatziki.

BASIC GREEK SAUCE
*2tbsp olive oil*
*1tsp white vinegar*
*1 clove garlic, peeled and crushed*
*225g/8oz Greek yoghurt*
*salt and pepper*
*1/2 cucumber, peeled and coarsely grated*
*2tbsp fresh mint, chopped*

VARIATION
*Omit the cucumber and mint from the recipe, then add the following:*
*2 spring onions*
*1dssp garlic chives, finely chopped*
*1/2 tsp paprika pepper*
*1dssp honey*

*Serves 4*

Beat the oil, vinegar and garlic together in a bowl using a fork. Add the yoghurt and salt and pepper, beat lightly until well blended and smooth, then add the flavouring. If making the lime traditional tzatziki, add the grated cucumber with skin removed, and the mint. Mix well and chill before serving.

## VARIATION

### SPRING ONION DIP
Add to the blended yoghurt, the finely chopped spring onion, chives and honey. Mix well together, then serve chilled.

# Mediterranean Way with Potatoes

Potatoes are popular throughout the world and every country has its own special way of cooking and doing things. Potatoes combine so well with any of the Mediterranean herbs, so choose whichever flavour you want, often determined by which dish they are being served with, e.g. potatoes with mint for lamb kebabs, fennel with fish or chicken, tarragon again with chicken or with basil if the accompaniment contains tomatoes or garlic.

*4–5 potatoes*
*1/2 onion, finely chopped*
*425ml/3/4pt cream or milk and cream, mixed*
*pinch salt*

VARIATION
*1dssp chives or parsley/tarragon, basil, rosemary*

*Serves 4*

Peel and dice or slice the potatoes, then arrange half into a greased, ovenproof dish. Sprinkle with half of the chopped onions and herbs. Then arrange the second layer of potatoes and sprinkle with the remainder of the onions and herbs. Pour over the milk and/or cream, cover with foil and bake in a preheated oven for 35–45 minutes at gas mark 6/200°C/400°F. The cooking time will vary with the thickness of the potatoes, but I find the thinner the potatoes, the tastier the dish.

NB This dish can also be made with yams or unpeeled potatoes.

# A Greek Country Salad

*4 plum tomatoes, sliced*
*1 red onion, sliced*
*8–10 black olives*
*115g/4oz Feta cheese*

DRESSING
*2dssp olive oil*
*1dssp balsamic vinegar*
*salt and pepper*

TO SERVE
*basil leaves, shredded*
*pinch cayenne pepper*

*Serves 4*

Arrange the sliced tomatoes and onions, olives and Feta cheese in a dish. Prepare the dressing by mixing together the oil, vinegar and seasoning. Pour over the salad and garnish with basil and cayenne pepper.

# Moussaka

Moussaka is one of the most popular dishes in Greece and, as with many dishes, it varies from region to region. It is not difficult to prepare, but it can be quite time-consuming. That is one reason why I have adapted the traditional version to my own Moussaka, which is made in a less time-consuming way, and topped with a yoghurt topping instead of a white sauce.

*1dssp olive oil*
*3 cloves garlic, chopped*
*1 large onion, coarsely chopped*
*450g/1lb minced lamb*
*salt and pepper*
*pinch cayenne pepper*
*2tbsp tomato purée*
*2–3 tomatoes, diced*
*1tsp oregano (fresh or dried)*
*2tsp parsley, chopped*
*140ml/¹/4pt red wine and 140ml/¹/4pt vegetable stock*
*or*
*280ml/¹/2pt vegetable stock*
*3–4 potatoes, peeled and cut into 1cm slices*
*2 aubergines, cut into 1cm slices*
*225g/8oz Greek yoghurt*
*2 egg yolks*
*115g/4oz cheese, grated (Mozzarella or Gruyère)*

*Serves 6–8*

Preheat oven to gas mark 5/190°C/375°F. Heat the olive oil in a large frying pan, add the garlic and onion and cook over a high temperature. Add the minced lamb and cook until browned. Add the salt, pepper, cayenne pepper, tomato purée, diced tomatoes, oregano and parsley. Mix well, then add the wine (if using) and stock. Cook until the liquid reduces, then begin to assemble the Moussaka.

In an ovenproof dish, layer the peeled, sliced potatoes, half the aubergines cut into slices (sprinkled with salt and left to sit for a short time to draw out the bitter juices). On top of this layer the lamb mixture and finally another layer of aubergines.

Mix the Greek yoghurt, egg yolks, half the grated cheese, salt and pepper together. Spread over the Moussaka, then sprinkle with the remaining cheese and dust with cayenne pepper. Bake in the oven for 45–50 minutes.

# An Aegean Salad & Salsa

Salsas are colourful, full of flavour and can be either hot and spicy or cool and refreshing. They appear very often in menus, a mixture of diced, grated or chopped fruit and vegetables, combined with a dressing. Salads, we are more accustomed to, yet when it comes to Greece, the typical ingredients common to both include aubergines, red onions, tomatoes, Feta cheese, olive oil and often oregano.

### A Warm Greek Salsa
*1 large aubergine*
*salt and pepper*
*1dssp olive oil*
*2 beef tomatoes*
*2 shallots*

### Dressing
*2dssp olive oil*
*juice of 1/2 lemon*
*1tbsp marjoram or oregano, chopped*

*Serves 4*

Slice the aubergine into rounds, sprinkle with salt and pepper, then brush with oil. Cut the tomatoes into slices, chop the shallots into 1" slices, then place all vegetables below a hot grill for 4–5 minutes, turning once. Cut the char grilled aubergines and tomatoes into large dice, add the roasted shallots and mix the dressing ingredients. Serve warm or chilled.

# The Versatile Aubergine

The deep purple aubergine with its egg shape, is the most popular one to cook. It should have a smooth, glossy skin and when cut, flesh that is fine textured and sweet. There are many ways to cook this interesting vegetable, but I find grilling one of the best. Remember to sprinkle the sliced aubergine with salt to remove the bitter juices and then cook on top of the grill pan, well brushed with oil. Grill for 1–2 minutes on either side then blot with kitchen paper to remove excess oil.

### Suggested toppings for aubergines

### Toasted Cheese & Bacon
*2tsp sun dried tomato paste*
*55g/2oz mozzarella or goat's cheese*
*1/2 tsp oil*
*black pepper*

*2 rashers streaky bacon, cut into strips*
*Serves 1*

Spread the cooked aubergine slices with the sun dried tomato paste, top with a round of cheese and sprinkle with oil and black pepper. Grill for 2–3 minutes, then serve hot, garnished with bacon strips.

### GARLIC & GRUYÈRE
*2 cloves garlic, finely chopped*
*115g/4oz Gruyère cheese, grated*

Sprinkle the aubergine with finely chopped garlic, then sprinkle on the grated Gruyère cheese. Grill for 2–3 minutes, then serve hot as a tasty snack.

# *The Greek Way with Fish*

From the Greek Islands comes an abundance of fish, many varieties of which we seldom see on our fishmonger's counter. Yet there are the ever-popular red mullet, gurnard, tuna and hake that we love to cook and eat, both at home and abroad. More and more the simple philosophy of 'the less you do with fish, the better it tastes' is encouragement to more people to cook fish. Whichever variety you are cooking, ask your fishmonger to fillet, scale and generally prepare the fish, so all that's left for you to do is to cook it. Keep to simple fish fillets, and either fry in olive oil and a bit of butter, or cook on a well-oiled grill pan until the fish becomes tender. Turn only once.

Here are two quick ideas to serve with fish, one sauce, and one salsa.

### FETA, OLIVE & TOMATO SALSA
*2 large, ripe tomatoes, diced*
*50g/2oz black olives*
*1 red onion, chopped*
*100g/4oz Feta cheese, cubed*
*1dssp olive oil*
*juice of 1 lemon*
*1tbsp parsley or coriander, finely chopped*

*Serves 2–3*

Place the diced tomatoes, olives, onion and Feta cheese in a serving bowl and toss well.

In a separate bowl, beat together the olive oil and lemon juice, then spoon over the salsa ingredients. Toss lightly, garnish with finely chopped parsley or coriander and serve.

### A GRAPE SAUCE
*1dssp olive oil*

*1 spring onion, finely chopped*
*55g/2oz green grapes*
*55g/2oz black grapes*
*1tsp white wine or balsamic vinegar*
*30g/1oz demerara sugar or*
*1dssp honey*
*1dssp parsley, finely chopped*

Heat the oil and gently fry the spring onion until just opaque. Add the grapes, white wine or balsamic vinegar, honey or sugar and parsley and bring to the boil. Serve at once with the grilled or fried fish.

NB  This sauce spoils very easily: if the grapes are overcooked, the colour becomes pale. Watch the temperature and cooking time carefully.

# Great Pudding Ideas with Greek Yoghurt

This luxurious tasting yoghurt has become so versatile in sauces, salsas and especially puddings. Reasonably low in fat content, it combines extremely well with cream or fromage frais to give the required texture. Use it to make a Very Berry Pudding topped with passion fruit or combined with Caribbean fruits such as mangoes, melons or paw paw.

FILLING
*450g/1lb soft berry fruits e.g. strawberries, raspberries, blueberries, currants or*
*450g/1lb assorted mangoes, melon, paw paw*
*30g/1oz demerara sugar*

BASIC YOGHURT SAUCE
*225g/8oz combination of Greek yoghurt, yoghurt, fromage frais*
*30g/1oz icing sugar*
*1dssp honey (optional)*

TO DECORATE
*1tsp demerara sugar*
*juice and seeds of 2 passion fruit*
*a few sprigs of mint*

*Serves 6–8*

Wash and prepare the fruits, then toss together in a serving bowl and sprinkle with demerara sugar. Prepare the topping by mixing together the yoghurt, fromage frais, icing sugar, half the passion fruit seeds and 1/4 of the prepared fruit.

Place the remainder of the prepared fruit into a serving bowl, and then pour over the yoghurt mixture, spreading over the fruits. Sprinkle with demerara sugar and the remaining passion fruit seeds. Serve decorated with a sprig of mint.

*Overleaf: A Very Berry Pudding*

# *Baklava*

Baklava is a very Greek tart made with layers of paper thin filo pastry, walnuts, honey and topped with a lemony syrup sauce. A delicious pudding that can be served with an extra helping of sauce, Greek yoghurt or cream. I have given two versions of this pudding. Firstly the sweeter, traditional version made with walnuts and a very syrupy sauce. The second, my own, less sweet version layered with sultanas, hazelnuts and cinnamon, topped with a lemony sauce.

TRADITIONAL BAKLAVA
*4 sheets filo pastry*
*15g/¹/₂oz butter*
*340g/12oz walnuts, chopped*
*30g/1oz demerara sugar*
*¹/₂ tsp cinnamon powder*

SUGAR SYRUP
*170g/6oz granulated sugar*
*280ml/¹/₂pt water*
*2tbsp honey*
*1tbsp lemon juice*
*2–3 cloves*
*¹/₂ tsp cinnamon powder*

*Serves 6–8*

Preheat the oven to gas mark 6/200°C/400°F. Brush each individual pastry sheet with melted butter, then arrange the sheets in a lightly greased 15–16cm/6–7" flan ring with the edges of the pastry overhanging the rim of the flan ring.

Prepare the filling by mixing together the chopped walnuts, sugar and cinnamon, then layer into the lined flan ring. Fold over the overlapping edges of pastry over the top and bake in the oven for 10–15 minutes until light, crispy and golden.

Make the sugar syrup by mixing together in a saucepan the sugar and the water. Boil until thick and syrupy, and then add the honey, lemon juice, cloves and cinnamon. Cook for a further 2 minutes, then cool slightly before pouring the reduced syrup over the top of the cooked flan.

# My Version of this Lemony Greek Tart

*4 sheets filo pastry*
*225g/8oz sultanas*
*55g/2oz hazelnuts*
*1dssp honey*
*15g/¹/₂oz butter*
*2dssp lemon juice*
*2dssp sherry*
*pinch cinnamon*
*peel of ¹/₂ lemon*

LEMONY SAUCE
*juice of 2 lemons*
*rind of ¹/₂ lemon*
*2dssp honey*
*30g/1oz soft brown sugar*
*1 stick cinnamon*

*Serves 6–8*

Preheat the oven to gas mark 6/200°C/400°F. Prepare the pastry in the same fashion as for the Baklava. Make the filling by melting the honey and butter together in a saucepan. Add the sultanas, hazelnuts, cinnamon, lemon and sherry. Stir well and leave to infuse for 10 minutes before spooning into the filo pastry case. Carefully fold the overhanging edges of pastry over the filling, brush with melted butter and bake in the oven for 10–15 minutes.

To make the sauce, pour the honey, lemon juice, lemon peel and cinnamon stick into a saucepan and heat gently. Cook for 5 minutes until bubbling and slightly thickened. Remove the cinnamon stick and serve drizzled over the fruit tart.

# The Flavours of France

T

he cuisine of France is renowned

throughout the world for its wealth of

sophisticated flavours and rich ingredients.

French cooking techniques and the French way of doing

things produce some of our favourite dishes: quiche, moules

marinière and cassoulet. Regional and national specialities

abound: the choice of cheese, wine, and dishes

with fowl or seafood is endless.

# A Few
## Special Ingredients

### TUILES

Tuiles are thin, little biscuits, often used as an accompaniment with ice creams, poached berries or crumbled over sorbets. These crisp almond biscuits are easily made. The almond mixture appears in many forms; in rolls, flat, thin biscuits or even shaped into baskets in individual patty tins, which can be filled with seasonal fruits.

### HERBES DE PROVENCE

In France, when herbs are out of season and fresh ones are not available, a mixture of dried herbs is used. This is a tasty combination of bay leaves, dried thyme, rosemary, summer savoury, lavender, cloves and orange zest. For the best flavour, herbs are picked in their prime and combined together.

### BAVAROIS

This delicious dessert is a mixture of *Crème Anglaise*, cream and gelatine blended together, chilled in the fridge until firm and then unmoulded. It is slightly firmer in texture than soufflé and can be flavoured with chocolate, vanilla, strawberry or raspberry. A hint of liqueur enhances the flavour.

# Puffed Up Soufflé with Bacon, Spinach & Cheese

The Soufflé has to be one of France's most popular and characteristic dishes. It can be made either hot or cold, with a variety of flavours and in many different ways. Some recipes give almost double value, in that the lightness of the soufflé can be re-heated in either the oven or under the grill, to puff it up for a second time. This basic recipe can be used with many flavours, although cheese, bacon and spinach are my favourites.

### CHEESE SOUFFLÉ MIXTURE
*45g/1<sup>1</sup>/2oz flour*
*30g/1oz butter*
*280ml/<sup>1</sup>/2pt milk*
*salt and pepper*
*pinch cayenne pepper*
*<sup>1</sup>/4 tsp mustard*
*2 egg yolks, lightly beaten*
*60g/2oz Camembert or Gruyère cheese*
*2 egg whites, stiffly beaten*
*30g/1oz walnuts or parsley*

### VARIATIONS
#### CHEESE SOUFFLÉ
*30g/1oz Camembert*
*Top the soufflé with small pieces of Camembert before placing under the grill.*

#### BACON SOUFFLÉ
*60g/2oz bacon, cooked and crumbled*
*Top the soufflé with cool, crumbled bacon, then re-cook*
*for the second time until puffed up again.*

#### SPINACH SOUFFLÉ
*120g/4oz spinach cooked and shredded*
*Fold the cool, shredded spinach into the soufflé before adding the egg white.*

*Serves 4*

Prepare the basic cheese soufflé mix by beating together the flour, butter and milk, mixing well to prevent the mixture becoming smooth. Bring to the boil, add the seasoning, cayenne pepper and mustard. Cool slightly, then add the beaten egg yolks and the cheese. When well mixed, fold in the stiffly beaten egg whites. Transfer to greased, individual ramekin dishes or a large soufflé dish. The dish can be dusted with finely shredded walnuts or parsley before filling with the mixture. Place the dish or dishes in a bain marie to prevent the soufflés overheating during cooking. Bake in the oven at gas mark 5/190°C/375°F for 20 minutes until well risen and firm. Cooking time for an individual soufflé may be slightly increased. When cooked, serve at once, or if turning into a twice-baked soufflé, turn out

*Overleaf: Puffed Up Soufflé with Bacon, Spinach & Camembert*

on to a greased baking tray and add the topping before baking again in the oven at gas mark 5/190°C/375°F, or under a grill until it rises up again.

# A Classic
# French Dressing

The most common dressing in France is the Vinaigrette, and today there are endless variations for preparation and serving. The oil may vary from olive to walnut or groundnut, and the vinegar from white wine to cider. Although French mustard is most commonly used, dried or whole grain mustard may also be used. I often warm the dressing gently to bring out the best of the flavour.

DRESSING
*4tbsp olive oil*
*1tbsp mild white vinegar*
*$^{1}/_{2}$ tsp mustard*
*1tsp caster sugar*
*1 clove garlic, crushed*
*salt and pepper*

*Serves 4–6*

To make the dressing, place all the ingredients in a bowl and whisk together until smooth and well beaten. For a more intense flavour, warm the ingredients for 30 seconds before serving. To vary this dressing add either diced, grilled bacon or roasted diced peppers.

## VARIATIONS

### BACON & WALNUT
Substitute olive oil with a mixture of olive and walnut oil, then add grilled, diced bacon to the dressing.

### ROASTED PEPPER
Grill a red and a yellow pepper until blackened and softened. Peel off the skin and add the diced pepper to the dressing.

# Simple Sauces
# for Magrets de Canard

Duck, as a rule, can be quite fatty, so I remove as much of the fat as possible before cooking, including the skin if it is breast alone to be cooked.

There are many ways to cook the breast, either grilled, poached or sautéed. I find the best way is to sprinkle the breast with salt and peppercorns, then place on a grill pan with oil and butter, cooking for 3 minutes on either side. Then transfer to the preheated oven at gas mark 6/200°C/400°F for 8–10 minutes. Serve sliced diagonally. Cooking time will depend on how well cooked you prefer duck: cook for 5 minutes if you like duck rare or 8–10 minutes if you prefer it well done.

### ORANGE SAUCE
*juice and flesh of 3 oranges, peeled and sliced*
*1dssp orange marmalade*
*1dssp sherry*
*30g/1oz brown sugar*

### BLACK CHERRY SAUCE
*400g/4oz can black cherries*
*1dssp cherry preserve*
*15g/1oz brown sugar*
*1dssp sherry*

Prepare the orange and the black sherry sauce by the same method. Place the fruit into a saucepan, add the preserve or marmalade, sherry and brown sugar. Heat together until bubbling and thickened, then serve.

### RHUBARB SAUCE
*70ml/¹/8pt water*
*30g/1oz demerara sugar*
*1 stick cinnamon*
*2 stalks rhubarb, sliced*
*1 cooking apple, sliced*
*30g/1oz demerara sugar*
*70ml/¹/8pt red wine*
*2dssp honey*

*Serves 2*

Place the water, sugar, cinnamon, rhubarb and apple in a small pan and poach gently for 4–5 minutes. Add the red wine and honey and cook for a further minute. Do not overcook. Serve hot.

# In a
# French Stew

Every country has its own special way of preparing a stew, and when it comes to France, the pot in which it is made is equally as important as the ingredients that go into it. 'Cassoulet', derived from the word 'casserole', is the earthenware pot used to cook the stew. Recipe variations are endless, with a range of ingredients from duck, goose, pork, bacon, onions, tomatoes and herbs all baked under a breadcrumb crust. This is my simplified version, adapted for more family-oriented tastes.

*450g/1lb haricot beans*
*570ml/1pt water*
*1 small carrot, chopped*
*1 onion, finely chopped*
*cloves*
*1dssp oil*
*680g/1½lb lamb, cut into large pieces*
*340g/12oz pork sausages, cut diagonally*
*115g/4oz garlic sausages, cut into chunks*
*340g/12oz bacon lardons*
*570ml/1pt chicken stock*
*2 onions, chopped*
*4 carrots, chopped*
*2 cloves garlic, chopped*
*salt and pepper*
*1 sprig rosemary, crushed*
*2 bay leaves*
*85g/3oz white breadcrumbs*
*2dssp parsley, finely chopped*

*Serves 6–8*

Steep the beans overnight in cold water, then transfer to a saucepan, cover with 570ml/1pt water, small piece of carrot, onion and a few cloves. Bring to the boil and simmer for 30 minutes, but do not allow them to become too soft.

In a large frying pan, heat the oil, then cook each meat separately at a high temperature until all the juices are sealed in and the meats are well seared. Transfer the lamb, pork sausages, garlic sausages and lardons of bacon in layers to a casserole dish.

Preheat oven to gas mark 5/190°C/375°F. To the pan in which the meats were cooked, add the chopped garlic, onions and carrots. Toss around for several minutes to coat the vegetables. Add a little salt and pepper, then transfer to the top of the meats. Add the crushed rosemary and bay leaf, sprinkle the beans on top and pour over the chicken stock. Place uncovered in the oven and cook for 1½ hours until the meats are tender when tested. About 15 minutes before the end of cooking time, remove the cassoulet from the oven, sprinkle with breadcrumbs and parsley and return to the oven, at gas mark 6/200°C/400°F for the remaining 15 minutes, or until the stew is golden brown on top.

# The French Way
## with Vegetables

Simplicity and style are the words which come to mind with the easy way to bring out the best of flavour with vegetables such as leeks, chicory and courgettes. The colour and flavour are intensified with the short cooking time. Here is a basic recipe for a cream sauce, and this can be varied by the addition of tarragon to leeks, parsley to chicory and coriander to courgettes. A delicious, simple way to bring out the true flavour of vegetables.

BASIC SAUCE
*280ml/¹/₂pt cream*
*15g/¹/₂oz butter*
*salt and black pepper*

FRENCH-STYLE LEEKS
*4 leeks*
*1dssp tarragon, finely chopped*

FRENCH-STYLE COURGETTES
*4 courgettes*
*1dssp parsley, finely chopped*

FRENCH-STYLE CHICORY
*4 chicory heads*
*1dssp coriander, finely chopped*

*Serves 6*

Prepare the sauce by heating together the cream and butter until the butter has melted. Add the salt and pepper and simmer for 1–2 minutes. Prepare the vegetables in a similar way. Wash and slice the leeks or courgettes, for the chicory, peel the leaves apart and shred coarsely.

Add the courgettes, leeks or chicory to the steamer and cook for several minutes. Drain well before adding to the sauce with the herb. Simmer for 1 minute, then serve hot.

# A
# Country Pie

Quiche Lorraine is a savoury open tart, which is ideal, served as a starter or as a main course. This traditional dish takes its name from a specific region of Lorraine and this type of pie has the main ingredients of eggs, cream and bacon, and often with onions and cheese, usually Gruyère. This pie can also be made with a variety of ingredients e.g. tomatoes, mushrooms, courgettes, spinach, fish and a selection of cheeses. My version of this classic pie is one which matches today's trend for recipes that are quick to prepare, healthier and cook in a flash. Choose from the suggested fillings and enjoy this pie, which substitutes the pastry with a crustless crumb.

### BASIC CRUSTLESS PIE MIXTURE
*170g/6oz self-raising flour*
*pinch salt and pepper*
*85g/3oz butter*
*55g/2oz bran*
*6 eggs*
*425ml/³/4pt milk*

### TO SERVE
*2dssp parsley, finely chopped*

*Serves 12*

## VARIATIONS OF FILLINGS

### RED ONION & PEPPER
*340g/12oz smoked bacon, cut into strips*
*2 red onions, chopped*
*1 red pepper, diced*
*salt and pepper*
*170g/6oz Gruyère cheese*
*2 tomatoes, diced*
*1 tomato, sliced*

Preheat oven to gas mark 5/190°C/375°F. Sieve the self-raising flour and salt into a large bowl, cut and rub in the butter, add the bran and mix again. In a separate bowl, whisk together the eggs and milk, then pour into the flour. Mix lightly, then add the prepared fillings and pour into a well oiled quiche dish 28–30cm/11–12" in diameter and bake in the oven for 25–30 minutes until firm, puffed up and golden.

Cook the bacon strips in a pan until crispy and golden, then add the onions, pepper and seasoning and cook for 1 minute. Turn off the heat and leave to cool. Add to the prepared flour and egg mixture, mix well then stir in the cheese, diced tomatoes and use the sliced tomato to decorate the top of the pie.

### CRAB & SPINACH
*225g/8oz cooked spinach, shredded*
*2 spring onions, finely chopped*
*85g/3oz Mozzarella cheese, grated*
*3dssp fromage frais*
*340g/12oz crab meat*

Lightly steam the spinach, drain and shred. Add the finely diced spring onions, grated Mozzarella cheese, fromage frais and cooked crab meat. Mix well before adding to the prepared egg and flour mixture.

# A Very Chic Tart
# with a Choice of Fillings

French pastry, with its rich, buttery taste is excellent for pies and tarts. Even though it is fragile and a little difficult to work with, I think you will find the finished result well worth the effort. If you relax the pastry in the fridge for a short time before rolling out, there is less chance of cracking. Use this pastry with any fruit, but I particularly like it combined with apples and hazelnuts or pears with almonds. Choose your favourite filling for this pie.

### PASTRY
*225g/8oz plain flour*
*15g/¹/₂oz caster sugar*
*pinch salt*
*115g/4oz butter, softened*
*1 egg yolk*
*1dssp cold water*

## FILLINGS

### APPLE AND HAZELNUT
*4 apples, peeled and sliced*
*115g/4oz butter*
*115g/4oz caster sugar*
*60g/2oz ground hazelnuts*
*30g/1oz whole hazelnuts, chopped*
*¹/₄ tsp vanilla essence*
*1 large egg beaten*
*45g/1¹/₂oz flour*
*1tsp cinnamon powder*

### PEAR AND ALMOND
*5 pears, peeled and quartered*
*115g/4oz butter*

*Overleaf: Crustless Quiche*

*115g/4oz caster sugar*
*1/4 tsp vanilla essence*
*70g/2<sup>1</sup>/2oz ground almonds*
*30g/1oz almond flakes*
*1 large egg, beaten*
*45g/1<sup>1</sup>/2oz flour*
*1tsp cinnamon powder*

TO SERVE
*30g/1oz icing sugar*
*1/2 tsp cinnamon powder*

*Serves 8–10*

PREPARE THE PASTRY
Sieve the flour into a bowl, add the sugar, salt and softened butter. Cut through, then rub in until it becomes almost sticky. Add the egg yolk, and if needed, water to bind together. Set aside to relax in the fridge or in a cool placed for at least 15 minutes. Roll out to fit a 22cm/9" loose-bottomed flan dish. Trim off any excess pastry, prick with a fork then set aside to relax before filling.

TO PREPARE THE FILLING
Poach the apple or pear gently for 2–3 minutes, if fruit is firm. Cream the butter and sugar together until white and fluffy, add the ground and chopped or flaked nuts, vanilla, egg and flour. Spread evenly over the pastry base, arrange the fruit on top and dust with cinnamon. Bake in the preheated oven at gas mark 5/190°C/375°F for 20–25 minutes until firm, golden and well cooked. Dust with icing sugar and cinnamon before serving.

# *Classic Creamy Sauces*

Sweet sauces are very popular with the variety of tarts and pies that are served throughout France, whether it's their classic crème Patisserie (pastry cream), crème Anglais (vanilla custard) or crème Chantilly, which is whipped cream flavoured with lemon, brandy, chocolate, coffee or orange. The great thing about all these sauces is that they can be prepared in advance, and will hold.

VANILLA CUSTARD
*570ml/1pt milk*
*1 vanilla pod*

*5 egg yolks*
*115g/4oz caster sugar*
*1tsp butter*
*rind of ¹/₂ lemon*

Heat the milk and the vanilla pod until almost boiling, then remove from heat. Beat the egg yolks and sugar until light and creamy, then gradually stir in the hot milk and return it to the heat. Bring up to simmering but not boiling point, until thick enough to coat the back of a spoon. Remove from the heat, add the butter and whisk in. Add the lemon rind and serve, either hot or cold.

## CHANTILLY CREAM
*140ml/¹/₄pt double cream*
*2tbsp ice cold milk*
*2tbsp icing sugar*
*¹/₂ tbsp vanilla essence*
*1tbsp iced water*
*rind of ¹/₂ lemon or alternative flavouring*

### ALTERNATIVE FLAVOURINGS
*chocolate – add 1dssp melted chocolate*
*coffee – add 1dssp cane coffee powder*
*brandy – add 1dssp white or black rum*
*rum – add extra 1tsp vanilla essence*

*Serves 6–8*

Place the cream and milk in a very cold bowl and whisk together until the mixture doubles in volume. This should take about 3–4 minutes. Add the sugar, vanilla flavouring, iced water and lemon rind, and continue to whisk for a further 1–2 minutes. To make a different flavour, add either chocolate, rum, brandy or coffee instead of lemon rind. Chill for 1 hour before serving.

# *Home Grown*

---

**S**almon, Potatoes, Bramley Apples, Fresh Fish and soda bread. When it comes to our own home grown produce then there's a lot we can be justly proud of, in quality, freshness and flavour.

# A Few
## Special Ingredients

### SALMON

Salmon or the king fish as it is often referred to is recognisable by the silvery blue streamlined body marked with spots. A most interesting fish as it spends half of its life in the fresh water and half in the sea.

When buying a whole salmon it should be firm, have a silvery sheen from the fish and have bright red gills.

There are many ways to cook salmon: poaching, grilling on its own or topped with butter, roasted, baked or in the microwave. Salmon is quite an oily fish with a high oil content, and in today's health conscious world oily fish rich in omega 3 are good for us.

### BUTTERMILK

My first memory of buttermilk was my grandmother's old-fashioned cure for sunburn. She believed that if it was spread over the sunburnt area it relieved the pain.

Its dietary uses today are endless. It is a by-product of the making of butter but today due to its wide demand it is made commercially. It is acidic with a sharp taste and works well with baking soda as a raising agent in the making of soda bread, scones and wheaten bread. I find it also gives bread a more savoury texture and keeps it fresh for longer.

### BRAMLEY APPLES

A world famous apple grown in the orchards of Armagh. Large, bright green and of the 'cooker' variety it is used widely in tarts, pies, sauces, muffins and cakes. It has a sharp flavour and a great texture to poach or bake and can be sweetened with sugar, syrup, honey or even maple syrup. Try spicing it up with cinnamon, cloves, nutmeg or even topping poached apples with roasted hazelnuts or almonds.

### POTATOES

I am of the firm belief that no one grows potatoes like the Irish. Today we are spoilt for choice as not only can we find endless main-crop varieties but types such as floury and waxy, each with their own special ways of cooking.

Whichever way you buy them, try not to store in a polythene bag, and you will find they keep better unwashed in the dark.

Champ is probably our most famous way of cooking potatoes with scallions, milk and melted butter added after cooking. But today because of their versatility we are finding so many new ways of cooking them, whether sliced, diced, baked, whole, roasted, cooked in a wok or flavoured with olive oil, bacon and chives for a bit of variety. Try champ with olives and chives for a real change.

# The Apple of My Eye Pie

Bramley apples have a unique flavour when used in an apple pie. Here they combine with cloves and orange, and are topped with a light almond crust.

*285g/10oz plain flour*
*¹/4 tsp baking powder*
*170g/6oz butter*
*1 small egg*
*30g/1oz icing sugar*
*1dssp milk*

FILLING
*3 Bramley apples, cut into wedges*
*6–8 cloves*
*2dssp crème fraîche*

TOPPING
*1 egg and egg white*
*30g/1oz caster sugar*
*15g/¹/2oz melted butter*
*30g/1oz flour*
*30g/1oz ground almonds*
*30g/1oz flaked almonds*

*Serves 8–10*

Pastry prepared in a blender is so much easier to deal with, and you end up with a pastry that is short and crumbly. Into the blender add the flour, baking powder, butter cut into pieces, icing sugar, lightly beaten egg and milk. Give the blender a short whizz until all the ingredients bind together. Be careful not to overheat the pastry, otherwise it will become very soft. Roll out the pastry to fit a 9–10" flan or loose bottomed dish. Relax the pastry for 30 minutes in the fridge before filling and baking for a short time, 10–15 minutes at gas mark 5/190°C/375°F. However, if the pastry is very freshly rolled, it may not require baking before filling, especially if you are cooking the pie in a dish with a perforated base.

Peel, core and slice the apples, then poach for 1–2 minutes in the orange juice, cloves and sugar then leave to cool before piling into the uncooked pastry case.

To make the topping, beat together the egg and sugar until light and frothy, then fold in the flour, butter, ground almond and half the flaked almonds. Spoon over the top of the pie. Sprinkle with the remainder of the flaked almonds, then cook in the oven at gas mark 5/190°C/375°F for 25 minutes approximately.

Serve hot or cold with yoghurt or a sprig of mint.

*Overleaf: The Apple of My Eye Pie*

# A Very Fishy
# Irish Stew

The best known of all our dishes has to be the Irish stew. Here is an interesting version for you, not made with mutton but for a bit of a change, with fish.

*680g/1¹/₂lbs white cod (or firm white fish)*
*2dssp lemon juice*
*1tsp black peppercorns, ground*
*1dssp oil*
*30g/1oz butter or polyunsaturated fat*
*1 small bunch spring onions, cut into strips*
*2 leeks, cut into chunks*
*425ml/³/₄pt milk*
*1–2 bay leaves*
*2 carrots*
*115g/4oz white beans (canned)*
*70ml/¹/₈pt cream (optional)*

To garnish
*2dssp parsley, finely chopped*

*Serves 6–8*

Sprinkle the fish pieces with lemon juice and black pepper and leave to sit for several minutes. In a large pan heat the oil and butter then lightly cook the spring onion and pieces of leek. Add the fish pieces. Toss lightly for several minutes then add the milk, bay leaf, carrots and beans. Poach gently for 10–12 minutes until the fish is tender, but don't overcook. Just before serving remove the bay leaf, add cream if desired, garnish with parsley and serve.

Be careful with this dish not to stir the fish otherwise it will break down and spoil the appearance.

Serve hot.

NB This dish can be made with any white fish but do be careful when buying it to choose firm, thick fleshed fish as this will cook better and not fall apart. Monkfish tails work a treat.

# Caramelised Cabbage
# with Onion

A rather tasty way to cook cabbage by steaming then caramelising in a pan with onions and honey.

*1 small green cabbage*
*1 Spanish onion, sliced*
*15g/1oz butter*
*1dssp honey*
*2dssp caramelised roasting lamb juices*

*Serves 4–6*

Steam the cabbage for 2 minutes then drain.

In a separate pan cook the onion slices in the butter, add the honey then the cabbage and finally the lamb juices. Cook for 1–2 minutes just heating through over a gentle heat. Then serve.

Be careful not to overcook the cabbage or the colour, flavour and food value will all spoil.

# Buttermilk Soda Scones with Bacon & Cheese

There is nothing quite like hot soda bread scones and when you combine them with lean bacon and cheese the flavour and texture are excellent. For a change, instead of rolling out the dough and cutting out with a cutter, shape into rounds and top with cooked bacon and either mozzarella or cheddar cheese.

*225g/8oz soda bread flour*
*pinch of salt*
*30g/1oz butter or polyunsaturated fat*
*55g/2oz bacon, lightly cooked*
*55g/2oz mozzarella or cheddar cheese*
*1dssp parsley, finely chopped*
*1 egg, lightly beaten*
*buttermilk*

*Serves 8–10*

Sieve the flour into a bowl, add salt, cut and rub in the fat. Grill the bacon for 2 minutes then cut into fine pieces and add to the flour along with the grated cheese and finely chopped parsley. Use the lightly beaten egg and buttermilk to mix together to a soft dough. Shape into 8 rounds, place on a floured baking sheet, brush with egg then lightly dust with a little cooked bacon and cheese.

Cook in the oven at gas mark 7/220°C/425°F for 10–15 minutes until golden, risen and cooked. Serve either hot or cold and lightly buttered.

*Overleaf: Buttermilk Soda Scones*

# Baby Potatoes with Lemon & Chives

*450g/1lb baby potatoes*
*30g/1oz butter or polyunsaturated fat*
*1dssp chives, coarsely chopped*
*¹/2 lemon (rind only)*

*Serves 4*

Wash and steam the potatoes for 12–15 minutes until tender. If preferred, they can be cut in half before cooking.

In a separate pan heat the butter, add the chopped chives and lemon, toss around to release the flavours, then pour over the potatoes and serve.

# Roasted Balsamic Beetroot

Beetroot with its vivid red colour and earthy flavour has to be one of our most underrated vegetables. In this dish I have served it hot with a dressing of warm balsamic vinegar and walnut oil.

*8–10 beetroot, fresh and unskinned*
*140–280ml/¹/4–¹/2pt water*

SAUCE
*4dssp walnut oil*
*2dssp balsamic vinegar*
*30g/1oz whole walnuts, shelled*
*salt and pepper*

*Serves 4*

Wash the beetroot well but do not scrub or tear the skin. The best way I find to cook them is in a roasting tin with ¹/4–¹/2pt water, cover with foil and cook until tender, approximately 1¹/2 hours at gas mark 3/160°C/325°F. When cooked, cut off the beetroot tops and bottoms, peel and dice into large chunks. To finish off: heat the walnut oil, toss in the diced beetroot, add the balsamic vinegar, a few whole walnuts and heat through. Season with salt and pepper and serve either hot or cold.

# Wild Irish Salmon Wrapped in Herbs

Wild Irish Salmon cooks beautifully whichever way you choose: grill, poach, bake or fry. In this recipe I have used the salmon fillets cut into strips or pieces lightly tossed in herbs and peppercorns then served in a light sauce spiced with paprika and textured with cucumber.

*680g/1¹/₂lbs salmon cut into chunks or strips*
*¹/₂ cup finely chopped herbs (parsley, basil, dill and fennel)*
*1dssp finely crushed peppercorns*
*30g/1oz butter and 2dssp oil*
*2dssp lemon juice*
*¹/₂ tsp paprika pepper*
*¹/₄ cucumber cut into strips*
*2dssp crème fraîche*
*2dssp yoghurt (or 140ml/¹/₄pt cream)*

To serve
*Garnish with lemon and lime twists*
*Paprika pepper*

*Serves 4*

Cut the salmon fillets into strips or chunks then toss in the chopped herbs. A variety of herbs can be used but I like the combination of flavours of parsley, basil and fennel. Use only a little fennel as it has a stronger aniseed flavour yet has the ability to bring out the flavour of fish. Sprinkle with lightly crushed peppercorns and pat down well. The oil in the salmon will help the herbs to bind to the salmon without the addition of any extra oil or egg.

Heat the oil and butter in the pan then carefully add the salmon pieces. Cook for 2 minutes on either side and only turn once or the fish will break up. When the salmon is almost cooked pour over the lemon juice, sprinkling of paprika pepper, cucumber peeled and cut into strips. Do not attempt to stir the salmon or it will break up. Add 2dssp of crème fraîche and 2dssp of low fat yoghurt and heat through for a further minute.

Garnish with lemon rind and paprika pepper. Turn off heat and just allow the sauce to heat through gently before serving.

This dish can also be cooked with trout. A combination of pink and white fleshed fish works well together, e.g. salmon and turbot, or trout with bull.

*Overleaf: Wild Irish Salmon and Baby Potatoes with Lemon & Chives*

# Roast Leg of Lamb
# with Fresh Herb Stuffing

There is still a great tradition here in Ireland, especially in rural areas, to serve a proper Sunday lunch and it's usually a roast. Here I have roasted lamb stuffed with a mild herb stuffing and topped with mustard and honey.

*1 leg of lamb, boned (3.6kg/8lb approximately)*

### STUFFING
*340g/12oz white breadcrumbs*
*1 small onion, finely chopped*
*1dssp oil*
*1 egg, lightly beaten*

### HERBS
*2 stalks rosemary (dried or fresh)*
*2 stalks fresh thyme (dried or fresh)*
*1 small bunch parsley, finely chopped (dried or fresh)*

### COATING
*1dssp mustard*
*1dssp honey*
*2dssp oil*
*1tsp thyme, chopped*

*Serves 10*

Get your butcher to bone the leg of lamb for you as it can be quite a tricky exercise.

Prepare the herbs. If using dried or frozen herbs there is no preparation required but if the rosemary and thyme are fresh then remove the leaves from the woody stems and chop very finely along with the parsley.

Lightly fry the onion in the oil for 1–2 minutes just until lightly softened.

Make the stuffing by mixing together the breadcrumbs, onion, herbs and egg and mix until the mixture starts to bind together. Pack the leg cavity with the stuffing then reshape and secure either with string or skewers.

Place onto foil then cover with mustard, honey, thyme and oil mixed together. Secure the foil loosely over the lamb then cook in the oven at gas mark 6/220°C/425°F for 30 minutes. Reduce temperature to gas mark 4/180°C/350°F for 25 minutes per lb, and allow an extra 20 minutes. Don't forget the standing time of 15 minutes before serving, to allow the meat juice to flow back through the lamb.

Serve with boiled or baked potatoes.

# Index

# Index

# Index

# Index

# Acknowledgements

I would like to acknowledge the assistance of the following people and organisations in both the making of the series, and the writing of the accompanying book.

The UTV television team: Ruth Johnston, Producer & Director, Alan Bremner, Controller Programming, Mike McCann, Head of Public Affairs; the crew: Sam Christie, Rai Woods, Ken McNally, Brian Armstrong and Mary McCleave.

The photography team: Robert McKeag, Howard Ward and Food Stylist Anne Bryan.

The team at Appletree Press: John Murphy, Publisher, David Ross, Marketing Director, Catherine McIlvenna and Claire Skillen.

To Maureen Best, Sally Stirling, Vera McCready, Joanne O'Neill and Linda McCrystal.

To Sally Backus, Floral Design Ballymena, for her fresh flower arrangements.

To David Flynn of Marlborough Antiques (Belfast); Nicholas Mosse Pottery (Kilkenny); Christine Foy, Mullaghmeen Pottery (Enniskillen); Michelle Kershaw, Lakeland Plastics; Habitat Belfast; Peter Nicholl, La Cucina Cookshops; Debenhams Belfast; Catherine McMillan, Beechgrove Interiors (Ballymena); John Cameron at Cameron's (Ballymena); Ken Crockett at Balmoral Flowers; Ian McKay, Calor Gas; DJ Lockhart, Platinum Homewares Lagostina; Cuisine Cookware and Le Creuset.

Finally, I would again like to thank everyone at UTV for their encouragement and support in both the television series and the writing of this book.

*Jenny Bristow*